IVAN THE TERRIBLE

Born: 1530
Died: 1584

The dramatic story of the first of the Czars, the strangely complex, tormented and towering figure known as Ivan the Terrible, began when he was proclaimed Ivan IV, Grand Prince of Moscow, at the age of three. His childhood was spent as a powerless pawn in the hands of warring nobles, and in this atmosphere of brutal treachery and ruthless ambition, he grew up to be morbidly suspicious and murderously vengeful. By the time of his death, he was absolute ruler of a realm that stretched from the Baltic to Siberia, and his name was known throughout the world. Filled with dreams of making Russia another Rome and himself a new Caesar, Ivan the Terrible more than any other man led Russia into the modern world.

BOOKS BY ALFRED APSLER

FIGHTER FOR INDEPENDENCE: Jawaharlal Nehru

IRON CHANCELLOR: Otto Von Bismarck

IVAN THE TERRIBLE

PROPHET OF REVOLUTION: Karl Marx

THE SUN KING: Louis XIV of France

Ivan the Terrible

by ALFRED APSLER

BAILEY BROTHERS AND SWINFEN LTD.
FOLKESTONE

Published by Bailey Brothers and Swinfen Ltd.

Copyright, ©, 1971 by Alfred Apsler

SBN 561-00113-8

To my daughter Ruby, whose valuable assistance
I deeply appreciate.

Printed in Great Britain by
Latimer Trend & Co. Ltd., Whitstable

CONTENTS

They openly confess that the will of the prince is the will of God, and that whatever the prince does he does by the will of God; on this account they call him God's key-bearer and chamberlain, and in short they believe that he is the executor of the divine will.

Baron Sigismund von Herberstein

1

BLOOD *in the* PALACE

The huge clapper swung back and forth, each time hitting the wall of the seventy-ton bell which hung exposed to all eyes in the bell tower, just under the golden, onion-shaped roof. Mournfully the sound floated from the Kremlin onto the square. It drifted across the winding Moskva River and lost itself in the dark-green forest beyond.

All Muskovites were assembled on Red Square, a public plaza which stretched clear across the small town from its east gate to its west gate. The inhabitants called it *Krassnaya ploshtshad,* and the Russian word *krassnaya* means not only "red" but also "beautiful."

It was a December day in 1533, and the frost bit through cloaks and boots, quite oblivious to the pale winter sun which hung seemingly lifeless in the blue-and-gray sky. Children played on the solid ice of the river or ran after the horse-drawn sleighs.

The usual commotion of merchants haggling over their wares was muted. The stalls which filled half the square were deserted; their owners stood around in groups, mingling with other townsmen in anxious conversation. Fur caps were drawn tightly over their ears and foreheads, and icicles glistened at the edges of their untrimmed beards.

"A sad day," remarked a fishmonger. "What will become of us now that the Grand Prince is dead?"

"God have mercy on his soul," answered a silversmith. He crossed himself, and those who stood near followed his example.

"We all need God's mercy now," said a peasant in a gray sheep's pelt who, like many others, had come into town for the day. "What will become of us now? The new grand prince is a child of three years. This may mean big trouble."

Heads nodded in sad agreement. The grand duchy of Moscow was in for grim times.

An old fur trader with a deeply lined, weather-beaten face summed it up: "We've had it before. The boyars will fight with each other over the regency, and their armed men will burn our huts and make sport with our daughters."

"And don't forget the Tatars," added another old-timer, a soldier with many scars to prove his former occupation. "As soon as they hear of the trouble, they will come raiding. Moscow will burn again as it has burned before. The monks had better light lots of candles to the Holy Virgin."

Gloomily they looked at the red-brick walls encircling the Kremlin. Those crenellated battlements, fifteen feet thick, had been built in prouder days by Ivan III, the dead ruler's father. Reinforced by several stout towers, they protected the Kremlin— a city within the city, a last refuge of Muscovites in times of dire need.

The people looked with pride at the Kremlin. The sight of its buildings inspired them with constant admiration. Three cathedrals rose, resplendent in white and red, topped by blue-and-gold domes, and around them crowded the princely palace, armories, stables and quarters of the serving men.

Finally the big bell fell silent. Vasily Ivanovich had been laid to rest in the Cathedral of the Archangel Michael. His coffin of stone, embossed with metal, now stood beside those of his ancestors near the high altar. Chanting black-robed monks, carrying long lighted tapers, led the mourners out of the cathedral. The solemn procession wound its way slowly between two lines of soldiers to the black-draped door of the royal palace. In the low vaulted throne room with the single stout column in the center, the boyars, Russia's proud nobility, seated themselves on backless wooden stools. They were broad-chested, well-muscled men, with features marked by battle and outdoor life. Slowly they took their places according to rank in an open rectangle, facing a high platform. The princes sat closest to the platform, and the boyars of lesser rank sat farther away. Their cloaks, trimmed with sable and ermine and laced with gold, fell to the stone floor, barely allowing a glimpse of their finely tooled leather boots.

Facing this spectacular assembly sat a little boy. Ivan Vasilevich, the fourth grand prince of this name, looked pathetic and slightly ridiculous with his short legs dangling from the oversized carved armchair. The pinched white face of the three-year-old child peeked forlornly from the fur-and-gold embroidery in which his whole body was swathed. On his tiny forehead rested a miniature crown, and his fingers, stiff and red from the frost, clasped a tiny scepter.

A group of priests advanced to the platform swinging censers from which rose a sweetish smell of incense. They flanked the Metropolitan, Joseph, highest churchman of the Russian Orthodox faith. Raising high a golden, richly bejeweled cross, he intoned: "God bless you, Ivan Vasilevich, Grand Prince of Moscow, Vladimir, Novgorod, Pskov, Tver and Ugorsk. May good fortune be with the great realm and with the throne of your father."

Then the Metropolitan turned to the glittering ranks of the nobility. One by one, the princes and the lesser boyars stepped forward. With bent knees they kissed the cross as a token of their pledge and swore fidelity to the new master. Each man also dropped a gift of fine cloth or jewelry at the child's feet.

Ivan was tired and cold, despite the fire of pine logs in the enormous chimney. The smoke stung his eyes. He had only a dim idea of what was happening, and he longed to be off at play with the other children of the palace. But as soon as he started to fidget, a stern look from the dark eyes of the handsome woman standing by his side made him resume his rigid posture. He did not want to displease his mother, the Grand Princess Helena, who looked very regal and very beautiful in her mourning attire. This was her first public appearance since giving birth to the late grand prince's second son, Yuri.

Finally the drawn-out ceremony was over. Ivan was now the ruler of a sizable territory, although he did not know where it began or where it ended. Servants took off his royal garments and stored them in heavy padlocked chests to await the next ceremonial occasion.

On that ominous day, the little prince could hardly have been aware of the threatening clouds on the political horizon, but it did not take long until even his young mind realized that something was terribly wrong.

His mother, Helena, was now regent. Under any circumstances this was no easy job for a woman in a land where women lived in oriental suppression. But additional difficulties made her task practically impossible. Her realm was in reality a loose confederation of duchies and principalities which had joined together only a short while before under the threat of foreign invasion. The various princes and dukes still regarded themselves as nearly independent masters of their own lands and bowed only grudgingly under the command of the Grand Prince of Moscow. They considered him their equal, not their superior. It was only an accident that had given the Muscovite prince the position of leadership, and they all felt equally entitled to play such a role.

At the time when feudalism was coming to an end in Western Europe, it had just reached full flower in the east. Boyars ruled the peasants on their estates without any restraint. They had their own contingents of armed men to enforce their dictates. Their code of honor forbade them to receive orders from anybody who was their inferior or even their equal, and this did not refer to ability, but exclusively to ancestry and to traditional rating.

If decisions concerning the whole country needed to be made, the nobility made them as a body, sitting in the Duma (council) of Boyars, but unlike the blue bloods west of the Alps, they had no code of chivalry which, at least in theory, kept the French or British knights from cutting each other's throats.

The attitude of the boyars towards their grand prince was: "You can have the honors as long as you leave us alone." Now, with a child installed in the Kremlin and with a woman ruling in his name, they expected more than ever to have their own way. To their general contempt for women was added a special dislike for this particular lady. She was a Lithuanian. The aging Vasili had sent his first wife to a nunnery because she could not bear him an heir. Then he had married a foreigner. "As if our Russian noblewomen were not good enough for him," grumbled the disappointed aristocrats.

Several close relatives were waiting eagerly to succeed the childless grand prince. But after expectations of a direct heir had almost vanished, little Ivan was born, dashing all hopes, especially those harbored by his uncles, Yuri and Andrei. Condemned to permanent subservience, the brothers of the late ruler plotted secretly against both the hated mother and her son.

But the princes and boyars had underestimated the imperious Helena. Once her son was installed as the grand prince, she displayed an iron determination to preserve the throne for her firstborn. Yuri and Andrei, who posed the gravest danger to her and her son's safety, were marked men. Soon both were arrested on a flimsy pretext. They died in prison. In the cold and damp dungeons below the Kremlin palace where the iron chains were heavy and the food scarce, life expectancy was notoriously low.

But even that was too slow a solution for Helena. There were always men looking for money or advancement who were willing to help her out of any predicament with the thrust of a dagger.

But the number of enemies was large, and it grew steadily. There were more arrests, more murders. Feelings grew more bitter with every passing week, and they reached a boiling point when it became evident that the widowed grand princess had a lover. Prince Ivan Obolensky rose suddenly from obscurity and took his place beside the regent. Together they handled the affairs of state.

In the ruling circles the rumors swirled about, thick as the winter clouds.

How long had this love affair been going on?

Was Ivan really the son of the late grand prince, who had been ailing and childless for so long?

The answer to all the insinuations was more arrests, more murders. Deeper and more vicious hatred resulted.

Five years after she had assumed the regency, Helena suddenly died. The talk of poison was loud and insistent. Often a potent drug, slipped into a goblet of wine, became the instrument of political ambition. But there was nobody to run down the rumors or, should they prove true, to bring the guilty to justice.

Ivan was eight years old. At the news that he had become a double orphan, the boy burst into tears and threw himself in the arms of Prince Obolensky. It was a pitiful and hopeless gesture. Bereft of Helena's protection, her lover managed to survive her by only a few months.

What the common people had feared when Vasili was laid to rest, now came with a vengeance. The duchy of Moscow lapsed into a state of anarchy. Hopelessly enmeshed in concerns of family rank and precedence, the nobility broke into rival factions, each bent on the complete destruction of all others.

Out of the general confusion emerged two powerful rival

clans, the Shuiskys and the Bielskys. Both claimed family ties with the deceased ruler. Both pointed to the exalted quality of their blood, to the glorious battles their ancestors had fought. Relatives and armed retainers rallied to the support of each clan, determined to settle the issue with blood, treachery, bribery or any other tool their power-thirsty imaginations could devise.

Back and forth swayed the struggle. Now a Shuisky captured the machinery of state, and the cries of tortured Bielskys echoed through the underground dungeons. Then the tables were turned. The dungeons were emptied of surviving Bielskys and refilled with Shuisky partisans. The gruesome process repeated itself several times.

All this happened only a few years after they had all sworn loyalty to the grand prince on the sacred cross. Now little Ivan was all but forgotten. Nobody paid any attention to the two orphan brothers. Reminiscing about his unhappy childhood, Ivan IV was to write later:

We and our brother were treated like foreigners, like the children of beggars; we were badly clothed, we were cold and hungry.

It was a life more suitable to the hovel than to the palace. Helpless and neglected, the two boys huddled in their quarters. They peered out of the slitlike windows, which were covered with fish bladders allowing some visibility, and wondered whether life outside was as gloomy as it was inside. Often the clash of arms and the cries of the wounded and the dying penetrated from the square below. Their eyes observed the unchecked ferocity of reckless men at arms. Corpses were left to rot in the mud. Merchant stalls were overturned and the merchandise scattered. Looters dragged away whatever they could carry. On the distant horizon rose the red glow of burning villages and monasteries.

Young as they were, the boys realized that their lives hung by thin threads. Only the fact that there was more than one pretender to the throne saved them. In the deadly power game the two little princes served as valuable pawns. Whoever was in the saddle at the moment, Shuisky or Bielsky, wanted possession of the grand prince's person, but they treated him as a prisoner rather than as their sovereign.

Many a night the boys woke up in terror when the violence spread from the streets into the numerous halls and stairways of the palace itself. Men, crazed with the thirst for blood, chased each other, breaking and slashing everything in their way.

Once a young officer bleeding from many wounds fled into Ivan's bedchamber. His pursuers followed at his heels with daggers drawn. The child tried to shield the fugitive with his little body, but rough hands shoved him aside. While he cowered in a corner shaking with fear, the man died at his feet, pierced by the daggers. Then the killers threw the corpse out the window.

All the combatants professed to be good Christians. But this did not prevent them from extending their violence to the highest representatives of the church. The manhunt continued. This time its victim was the Metropolitan, Joseph, who had incurred the disfavor of the Shuisky clan. A mob hurled stones at his residence. His robes torn and blood-spattered, he fled into the grand prince's sleeping quarters. There he was cornered and cruelly knocked about in Ivan's presence. But this time, they listened to the boy's pleading, and the Metropolitan managed to escape. Ivan called for a troika, a sleigh with three horses, and the prelate fled in haste into exile, pursued by the laughter and the curses of young nobles.

Back in Ivan's room, Prince Andrei, leader of the Shuiskys, sheathed his dagger. He had led the chase of the Metropolitan. Tired and perspiring, he sank onto a stool and propped his booted feet on the bed.

Ivan jumped forward. Hot indignation suddenly overcame his fear. "Get off that bed," he shouted, "or you will be sorry. My father died in this bed."

The boyar leader only made himself more comfortable. Tears of helpless fury streaked the child's pale cheeks.

Only a very few people took the trouble to give Ivan any kind of attention, and they had a habit of disappearing unceremoniously. Prince Obolensky died in prison from hunger and from the weight of his chains. The servants who were allowed near the little prince were carefully selected spies in the service of either the Shuiskys or the Bielskys.

In Agrafena, a kindly nurse, Ivan sought a little of the tenderness which a child expects from a mother. But one morning, as Agrafena came to dress him, he saw that her eyes were red from a night of crying.

"I have to say good-bye to you now, my darling," she sobbed. "I have been ordered to leave Moscow today."

"I order you to stay," shouted the child. "I love you. They can't take you away from me, I am the grand prince." But his words carried no weight, and Agrafena disappeared from his life.

The very walls of the Kremlin palace seemed to breathe hostility. Horrors lurked in every corner. Only during the height of summer, when the boys were taken to the summer residence, was the atmosphere less strained. There they lived peacefully in a comfortable cottage deep in the forest. For a short while they felt secure.

Ivan loved the forest, deep, dark and mysterious, and the steppe beyond—the land of waving grass where millions of flowers sparkled in yellow, blue and purple. He felt at home in this, the cradle of Russia, where the endless forest of the north meets the endless steppe of the south. Here was the wealth and strength of his realm, the duchy of Moscow.

But the balmy summer days had to come to an end. Back in the Kremlin his days passed again in fear and loneliness. Then he found a companion in Fedor Vorontov. This rare member of the boyar class defied the leading princes and took his oath of allegiance seriously. He spent time with the boys, and Ivan clung to him as to the father he had never known. Fedor soothed him to sleep with stories of ancient heroes, and listened patiently to the confidences of the child.

But punishment came swiftly. The Duma of Boyars was in session. On such occasions they remembered the grand prince. He was brought from his remote corner of the palace, clothed in his formal robes and placed on the elevated platform. Quickly the boyars made their formal obeisance to the sovereign, but as soon as they unbent their knees, they went about their business as if he had ceased to exist.

They engaged in their usual bitter quarrels, shouting curses at each other at the tops of their lungs. Fedor Vorontov stood near the dais. Under some pretext, Andrei Shuisky suddenly turned on him and attacked him in violent language. Before Fedor could gather his wits, the whole Shuisky clan was upon him, shouting and punching. They struck him from all directions until he stumbled and fell to the floor. Ivan jumped from his seat to protect his friend, but several pairs of hands grasped him roughly and kept him away.

After receiving a cruel beating, Vorontov was allowed to escape. To save his skin, he fled to the farthest corner of the grand duchy. Like Agrafena, Vorontov disappeared from Ivan's life. Loneliness closed in, more depressing than ever.

So began the rule of Ivan IV. The experiences of those early years burned themselves deeply into his memory: the ceremonial reverence accorded him on formal occasions, when he was brought out to play the role of the sovereign and the neglect, and the contempt which he encountered on all other days. He became a brooding child, filled with fear and mistrust, cynical at an early age, ready to think the worst about anybody who crossed his path.

In those unhappy childhood years can be found the key to the character of the man whom the world was to know as Ivan the Terrible.

2

LINKS with the PAST

What happens to a child's mind when it is continuously exposed to violence? Can anyone be surprised when such a mind regards crude barbarity as standard behavior?

Grand Prince Ivan needed companions his own age. There was, of course, his younger brother, Yuri, who followed him around like a faithful pup. But it became clear, almost from the day of Yuri's birth, that this second son of Vasili was slow-witted, a harmless, mentally retarded creature.

Ivan, an active and restless youngster, found a few playmates among the sons of clerks, armorers and servants who had their living quarters within the Kremlin enclosure. Their games were wild, but when they wrestled and raced, the little grand prince was always allowed to be the winner. They bowed to his command and accepted all his suggestions without protest. Among the small fry, at least, his rank was respected.

One of their favorite games was chasing the many dogs around the palace, fine hunting hounds as well as nondescript mongrels. Occasionally the band of loudly screeching boys caught one of the four-legged creatures by the ears or by the tail. At Ivan's command they dragged the victim up to the top of a watchtower. They crowded onto the narrow gallery which encircled the top of the tower. "Let go," shouted the prince, with an imperial wave of his hand, and the dog went sailing down to crash bloodily on the stone ground below.

The hardened men-at-arms who watched this pastime from their sentry stations only laughed. None of the boyars who happened by raised any objection. Let the boy have his fun, they reasoned, as long as he does not interfere with our plans, with our power game.

A youth raised on such fare could easily grow into a mindless brute. But this was not the case with Ivan IV, Grand Prince of Moscow. Though marked for life by the cruelty which surrounded him from his earliest days, he developed into a highly complex and, in many ways, extraordinary person.

The man who changed him from just a butcher of helpless animals to a youth of superior mental capacities was his spiritual guide, the new Metropolitan of Moscow.

Metropolitan Macary was an outstanding scholar in a society where scholarship was barely in its infancy. He laboriously collected books among a population which was mostly illiterate. This meant a continuous search for the parchment scrolls kept in monasteries and in the treasure chests of the larger churches. From those meager sources Macary compiled a somewhat confused account of sacred and secular history.

Macary was, for a long time, the only adult to pay any attention to Ivan's mental development. There were no schools even for children in the highest social circles, and so the Metropolitan made it his personal task to supervise the ruler's education. Soon he discovered that the boy was gifted with unusual intelligence. Once exposed to learning, Ivan displayed an eager curiosity which was supported by an amazing memory.

Ceremonial and administrative duties required much of Macary's time. Since he did not want to neglect the promising mental development of his pupil, he brought in Sylvester, a priest, who became Ivan's chief tutor.

Guided and prodded by the two churchmen, Ivan soon mastered the arts of reading and writing. All through his life he maintained an amazing skill in written and oral expression in his native tongue, the Great Russian language. (Great Russian belongs to the Slavic family of languages and is very similar to the White Russian and the Ukrainian which are spoken in other parts of what is today the Soviet Union, a state composed of many different nationalities. Because of the country's turbulent history, the Russian language and its relatives have absorbed many Greek, Mongol and Arabic terms.)

Ivan became an avid reader, but unfortunately for his talent, there was not much to read. His mind remained underfed, his intellectual capacity underdeveloped.

In Western Europe this was the time of the Renaissance and the Reformation. Luther and Calvin boldly challenged long-acknowledged religious concepts. In their witty and erudite writings, Montaigne and Rabelais exposed human weakness and hypocrisy. At the same time, Leonardo da Vinci and Michelangelo reached soaring heights of artistic creativity, and modern science began to transform man's capacity to control nature. Geographers drew a new picture of the planet earth, and brave men set out in perilously little sailing ships to explore it to its farthest reaches.

But the Russian giant continued to sleep. The great novels and poems the Russian genius was to produce were still unwritten, its haunting music still uncomposed. Locked in ignorance, its spirit was waiting to be awakened.

Ivan's reading list consisted exclusively of religious writings. In their cells, monks had laboriously copied and recopied the books of the Bible and the pious legends about miracle-working saints, among whom were supposed to be several of Ivan's ancestors.

He buried himself deeply in these dusty chronicles, a curious mixture of legend and historical truth, all served up with the devout frosting of a fanatic faith. The past of Russia was depicted as a product of God's will, the victories as miraculous rewards for its piety, the defeats as just punishment for its sins and pagan aberrations.

All this unfolded itself, devoid of any critical judgment, without any clear conception of times and places. Biblical prophets became the ancestors of classical heroes who, in turn, sired the chief Muscovite warriors.

So Ivan read about Noah and the great flood, about David and Nebuchadnezzar. The chronicles jumped to Alexander the Great, who was followed, in short order, by Caesar Augustus, master of the glorious Roman Empire. The unknown authors invented a mythical brother of Augustus, by name of Prus, whose descendants were the Ruriks, the first princes to rule over a Russian state.

Ivan was told that he was a Rurik. Thus he believed that his family was directly linked by a blood relationship with the biblical personalities and with the great Caesars who ruled a mighty empire from their magnificent capital, Rome.

If better-trained teachers and more accurate textbooks had been available to the student, they would have taught him that such connection with ancient Israel and Rome existed only in the imagination of certain monks, untrained in systematic research and in logical reasoning.

Classical Rome had long since lost its luster. Its line of emperors was already extinguished when, in the ninth century, the Varangians, a tough breed of Northern European warriors and traders, moved from Scandinavia and the Baltic seacoast up the Dvina and down the Dnieper River into the Ukraine. First they subjugated the native Slavic population, and then they intermarried with it. Their trading post of Kiev grew into a proud city, and in time it became the capital of the first kingdom on Russian soil, ruled by the Rurik dynasty, which was probably of mixed Norse and Slavic origin.

The city of Rome was now a head without a body, having lost its empire, and its heir was Constantinople, the brilliant metropolis by the Black Sea and the capital of the Byzantine Empire. It was not from Rome, but from Constantinople, that the bloodstream of the new Russian nation received its cultural nutrients. The Byzantine Empire formed a bridge from Europe to Asia. It stretched from the shores of the Adriatic Sea, across Greece and deep into the lands east of the Mediterranean. On the soil where Socrates and Plato once taught was preserved the classical heritage, enriched by the ways and the thoughts of the Middle East.

Byzantium gave Russia its written alphabet, its architectural style and its ostentatious ceremonials. From there also came the brand of Christianity to which Ivan clung throughout his life with a devotion which bordered on fanaticism.

It was not from Rome, but from Constantinople, that missionaries fanned out to convert the pagan Russians. They established a branch of the Greek Orthodox Church to the north of the Black Sea and thereby raised a wall of distrust that was to separate Eastern Europe from the Roman Catholic West for many centuries to come.

Wooden churches which imitated the Byzantine style of sacred architecture began to dot the clearings in the endless Russian forest. Monk artists, often of Greek birth, painted icons, the holy pictures of Christ and the saints. In solemn, lifeless rigidity, these images stared from their golden backgrounds at the believers who kissed them and prostrated themselves before them in awe and reverence.

Bearded priests in golden vestments staged highly theatrical religious ceremonies full of an elaborate pageantry which deeply impressed the traders of Kiev and the pioneers who chopped islands of fertile farmland out of the dense forest.

The Russian Orthodox priests were married, and they refused to pay homage to the Pope in Rome. In a purely ceremonial way, they acknowledged the leadership of the Patriarch in Constantinople, but in reality their chief official was the Metropolitan, who presided over a practically independent Russian church. His seat was in Kiev at first.

Eagerly Ivan tried to make sense of the confused and often contradictory chronicles. He was particularly fascinated by the role which the Byzantine emperor played. In the splendor and languid luxury of Constantinople he ruled as the absolute master of his realm. In the eyes of his subjects he ranked only slightly below God Himself. Nobody attacked his exalted position, least of all the church.

Though the Patriarch of Constantinople was honored as the foremost churchman in the Eastern Orthodox world, he was no pope, but a servant of the emperor. He never challenged the authority of the throne as medieval popes had done repeatedly. The emperor was the real head of church as well as state. His mandate, it was believed, came directly from the Lord, and to oppose him or even to talk of him disrespectfully was a sin akin to blasphemy.

Ivan was deeply impressed by this picture of a near-divine monarch. This was how a ruler should be treated, how he, Grand Prince of Moscow, should be regarded by his subjects. But the gap between the ideal and reality disturbed him deeply. How miserable his own position looked compared with all this monarchic grandeur. Even more than before he resented his helplessness, the indignities he had to endure even in his own residence. What a humiliating contrast to the luster of the Byzantine throne. As long as he lived, he was to strive for the magnificence that surrounded the court of Constantinople, and he never forgot that, in his youth, he had to swallow treatment which in Byzantium would have been unthinkable, even for the remotest cousins of the monarch.

But the old chronicles did not end there. As he continued reading, he was shocked to find that this dazzling pageant of

Byzantine royal dominance had ended many decades before he was born. The curtain had rung down on the great drama; its final act had been stark tragedy. There were no more near-divine emperors in Constantinople. The last bearer of the illustrious title had fallen in the final battle against a Muslim invader, and a shudder had gone through the whole Christian world.

From the distant steppes of Turkestan, they had poured into the highly civilized regions of Persia and the Middle East. In cities rich with ruins of an even more glorious past, they paused to take on the faith of Islam, submission to Allah, the Almighty, and to the message of Muhammad, His Prophet. Recruiting more soldiers from the lands they had overrun, they moved on, piercing the thinly guarded outer limits of the Byzantine Empire.

Horror struck the ranks of Eastern Christendom. Their sins must have indeed been shocking to the eyes of God, for He granted victory to the infidels, the Ottoman Turks. On a dark day in 1453, the last Byzantine emperor lost his life in battle and the green banner of the Prophet was planted on the ramparts of Constantinople, the pearl on the Bosporus. Down came the golden cross from St. Sophia's Basilica, the largest and most august temple of Christianity. The Turkish Sultan caused several tall spires to be erected around its powerful dome, and from their top galleries sounded the Muslim call to prayer: "There is no god but Allah, and Muhammad is His prophet."

Ivan read and reread the account many times, and still he could not grasp how God could have let this happen. He pondered about it in solitude. Where was divine justice? Why were the cursed infidels allowed to remain victorious? Why was the greatest shrine of the "true church" defiled by the hands of unbelievers?

At length he talked over his doubts with his tutor, Sylvester. Together they arrived at an answer.

"It was all God's plan," maintained the priest steadfastly, "even though we may not understand its purpose."

"I think I can see the outlines of the plan," Ivan said, his usually pale cheeks now red with fervor.

"You, lad, can guess at the meaning of divine providence?"

"It's no guess, Father. It must be. so. Constantinople died because its inhabitants had gone slack. They were steeped in sin and immorality, and so they had to perish. But God saw that it was time that another city arise, another center for our faith."

Sylvester regarded the boy with growing wonderment. There was something like prophetic fire in the young voice, and soon the priest, himself given to mystical, emotionalized expression, caught the spirit.

"Yes, my prince. Your words have the ring of divine truth. I can see it. There was Rome, where the church had its beginning. But the bishop of Rome strayed from God's path. So Rome fell, and Constantinople arose, the Second Rome. Now the proud pearl of Byzantium has been trodden into the dust, and Christendom is waiting for the Third Rome to rise. There is only one place where the Third Rome can rise—right here, for the Russians are now left as the main host of our faith."

"Moscow, the Third Rome; Moscow, the Third Rome." The boy's eyes shone as he repeated the words over and over. He had completely forgotten where he was and with whom.

When Sylvester was gone, and Ivan looked out upon Red Square, his mind returned to reality. The setting sun turned the brown dust into scarlet red for an instant, and merchants scrambled out of the way as a band of boyars rode from the Kremlin gate.

The boyars! Ivan saw it clearly—there could be no Third Rome until the boyars had learned to obey. And aside from those arrogant nobles there was yet another obstacle that had to be torn down before the great dream could come true: the Tartars still had their dreaded curved daggers aimed at the heart of Moscow.

In the thirteenth century, a catastrophe had overtaken the Russian tribes and cities, one more dreadful and more deadly than anything that befell the capital on the Bosporus. Another tribe of heretofore-unknown Asian nomadic steppe-dwellers went on the rampage. Within a few decades, they became the most terrible and the most successful conquerors the world had ever seen or was to see in centuries to come.

The Tatars, some of Mongol and some of Turkish origin, were tough riders on wiry little horses. They left their herds and their black tents of hide spread out near Lake Baikal and gathered around their leader, Genghis Khan. Their clothes of undressed animal skin hanging loosely over their short bodies, they followed this genius of military strategy as he dispatched their armies, led by his sons, towards the east, the south and the west. Never had the world witnessed such stunning victories. Mongols conquered China, Mongols smashed into India and still other swift-riding Tatar hosts pushed into Europe until they could water their horses in the Danube not far from Vienna. No force of knights in armor could have withstood the invaders had they set their minds on continuing all the way to the Atlantic Ocean.

The glow of joyful anticipation was gone from Ivan's cheeks, and deep gloom caused big tears to wet them as he unrolled more of the wrinkled parchments which told of Tatar victories and of Russian humiliation. This was where the past blended into the present.

He dropped the scrolls to the dusty floor and mounted one of the watchtowers. He looked into the distance, and in his vivid imagination he beheld lines of riders, their heads barely visible above the tall grass, the horse-tail insignia carried high in front of them.

As far as he could see, the land was flat—forest, marshes, grassland. He had heard that this seemingly limitless plain reached, uninterrupted, from the Arctic Sea in the North to the Black Sea in the South. But as to its east-west expansion, he only knew that it was staggering, without end. So, at least, it appeared to his searching eye.

Actually the plains extended from the eastern foothills of the

Alps across the bulky landmass of Eastern Europe to the Ural Mountains. But this range, which traditionally marks off the European continent from Asia, forms only a small obstacle, and beyond it the plains sweep on through the width of the giant Asian continent.

Rivers flow lazily north or southward, forming a parallel design of arteries which bring lifeblood to the world's largest reservoir of pine, birch and lime trees. In summer it is tinted with different shades of green. But during the long months of the deadly Russian winter, it lies buried under a glaring blanket of snow while the rivers transform themselves into snakelike bands of thick ice.

From his high perch Ivan could glimpse only a tiny segment of this world which had been overrun by the Tatars. Nothing could resist the lightning raids of the thick-set, slit-eyed men with their clean-shaven skulls and long, drooping mustaches.

For about two centuries, the existence of an independent Russian community was blotted out. Kiev lay in ashes. The Tatar rule left indelible imprints on the land and its people. Tatar words slipped into the Russian language, and Tatar customs and ideas slipped into the Russian way of life. The blood of conquerors and conquered intermingled. All this raised even higher the invisible barrier which separates Russian attitudes from those of their neighbors to the west.

Gradually Genghis Khan's enormous empire split into several parts, but even the splinters were still formidable domains. One of them, that of the Golden Horde, ruled over what was later to become Russia. Now the son of Grand Prince Vasili saw why the third Rome could not arise immediately after the second was drowned in the Turkish flood. It could only be a dream as long as the Russian people were nothing but captives of the Golden Horde.

European writers, having naturally little sympathy for the Mongol invaders, have often described them as brutal savages and nothing more. Savage they were, according to the stories and rumors that preceded them everywhere. Any resistance, real or suspected, was punished by wholesale massacres of men, women and children. Entire sections of the country were laid waste. Compassion and mercy were concepts incomprehensible to the Tatar khans. But when not in the process of eliminating enemies, they proved to be skilled administrators, and they knew how to copy successfully the ways of the conquered, such as the record-keeping of the Chinese or the commerce carried on over the old Silk Road leading from the Far East to the Mediterranean. In fact, trade blossomed under Tatar rule as it never had before; the trails were protected, and nobody dared to break the *Pax Tatarica* (Tatar peace).

The khans extended post roads from river to river, with relay stations spaced at intervals of a day's journey. On these roads swift ponies carried the khan's messengers and the inspectors who exacted tributes of fur, honey and grain. Failure to deliver the whole measure of what the khan demanded brought swift retaliation. Fields and houses were burned, men slaughtered, women and children carried off to be sold into slavery to Turkish or Venetian merchants.

The Russian farm- and pastureland belonged to aristocratic families. Once proud and practically independent, they had become tributaries, practically hostages of the khan. When his representative came riding in state, surrounded by guards with bows and arrows on the ready, the Russian nobleman had to meet him humbly outside the village. On foot he approached the mounted emissary and offered him a bowl of mare's milk as a sign of submission. Then he led the Tatar's horse by the bridle to his quarters as if he were a slave.

In Sarai, on the lower Volga, stood the capital of the Golden Horde. It was not so much a city as a giant camp of yurts, the mobile Mongol tents. In the center stood the khan's yurt, domed, covered with gold and brocade and hung with gorgeous oriental tapestry on the inside.

Every Russian prince, every boyar who possessed a village or two with a few hundred peasants in them, knew that he held his position only as long as it pleased the khan. To gain or retain his favor they traveled to Sarai, jostling each other for recognition, acting as spies and informers on their own kind, trying to outdo one another with costly presents. They even brought their sons to be kept as hostages and their daughters to be left in the harems of Tatar officials. Survival had to be bought at any price.

When Ivan reached this phase of Russia's troubled history, he ceased to rely on the written chronicles of half-literate monks. This ignominious period was still fresh in the minds of the older people, who had heard about it from their fathers and grandfathers. Strolling entertainers sang about it in the marketplaces and in the taverns.

These had been dark centuries for the Russian people, but they also marked the beginning of Moscow's rise to greatness. Ivan's capital on the Moskva River was at first no more than a waystation in the nearly trackless forest wilderness. Fugitives from the Tatar onslought built a few log cabins. More pioneers arrived. Driven from the old trade centers of Kiev and Novgorod, merchants began to float their barges down the winding Moskva. In the hamlet which nestled in the river bend they found rest and a market for their much-needed wares. What they did not sell to the few Muscovites they could carry by short overland portage roads to the Volga, Oka and Dnieper Rivers.

Ivan's ancestors, strong-willed warriors who made dubious claims to descent from the Rurik dynasty of Kiev, built the first Kremlin. There the refugees found welcome shelter, and in return they acknowledged the Rurik dukes as their overlords.

Still the Moscow rulers were only very minor princes hardly known beyond a day's ride. Dutifully they sent tribute to the khan, who then left them to their own devices. In time they were even allowed to act as collectors of tribute themselves. What they exacted from peasants, merchants and lesser nobles, they passed on to their Mongol masters under the watchful eyes of Tatar commissars and their Chinese accountants.

The shrewd Moscow princes used their good standing with the khans to amass more land and more subjects. Copying Tatar methods, they reached out in all directions, subjugating neighboring duchies and filling their stout hardwood chests with whatever treasures they could conceal from the keen eyes of the Tatar emissaries and from the Russian spies in their pay.

Growing in wealth and strength, the princes of Moscow bided their time behind their wooden ramparts. Finally the Tatar hold began to weaken. The once lean nomads of the steppe waxed fat in Kazan and Astrakhan, rich caravan stops which had grown into wealthy towns. Dissension rent the ranks of the Golden Horde, and it broke into fragments, which fiercely warred among themselves.

Moscow saw its chance, and the man who boldly took it was Ivan's grandfather, his revered model and the ancestor for whom he was named. Historians often accord him the by-name "the Great." Ivan III let it be known that from then on he would send no further tribute to Sarai, and he got away with it. His estimate of Mongol weakness proved correct.

With this intrepid act of defiance, Ivan III announced to the world that Moscow was an independent state. The arrival on the scene of a new political power was further dramatized by his marriage to Sophia Paleologue, niece of the last Byzantine emperor, the same one who had given his life in a vain attempt to keep the Turks from conquering his empire. The house of Rurik was now linked with the dynasty which had ruled the Second Rome. The outline of the Third Rome on the Russian plain was taking shape.

A new Russia was rising out of the ashes of Mongol destruction, dominated no longer by Kiev on its western flank, but by the wooden city in its heartland near the mighty Volga and its tributary, the Oka.

With all the enthusiasm of a boy thirsting for adventure, Ivan listened to the stories extolling the deeds of his ancestors, embellished as they had become by constant telling and retelling. There was his forbear Dmitri, Donskoi, the hero of Kulikovo Field, where, for the first time, Muscovites had defeated a Mongol army. It was by no means a decisive victory, but the halo of invincibility had been stripped from the dreaded horsemen. They were human, after all, and they could be put to flight by a combination of cunning and courage.

Grandfather Ivan had extended Moscow's rule over many neighboring principalities, and Vasili, the father whom he had hardly known, had continued to subdue Russian princes who exhibited less skill and fighting spirit.

And so here he was, Ivan IV, heir to a glorious beginning. Strongly he felt it his mission to carry on what his ancestors had initiated. But how? At the moment he was a helpless hostage handed back and forth among feuding boyars.

Lonely and powerless, he dreamed of his destiny, the mission of founding the Third Rome. So far the principality of Moscow was only a shadowy skeleton without muscle and flesh, a piece of earth without defined boundaries, still under constant threat from the outside.

Though divided and warring among themselves, Tatar raiders continued to menace the countryside. When their spies reported the infighting of the nobles and the general confusion in the streets of the main city, horses were untethered in the yurt camps, and eager men sharpened their curved daggers.

Messengers appeared in Moscow bringing violent threats. The frightened boyars sent back emissaries bearing costly gifts to appease the raiders, but this only whetted Tatar appetites. They were not after permanent conquest, but after loot. Through trackless prairie land they rode, with the high grass reaching almost to the eyebrows of the riders, or they trekked on the thick ice of frozen rivers. Burned villages, abandoned by all living creatures, marked their progress.

"Everything was barren," reports an eyewitness, "for eighteen miles before the town of Moscow." In 1540 Russian scouts reported that the advancing hordes were so numerous that they stretched beyond the horizon of the steppes. Fear bolstered imagination, and Moscow was in panic.

In fear of life and possessions, the people looked to their young grand prince. When he showed himself on the square, they clung to the hem of his clothing. "Help us," they cried. "Save us. Lead us against the enemy as your grandfather had done." He was their charm, their mascot, their hope.

Seeing him on ceremonial occasions paraded in royal splendor, the arrogant boyars holding the stirrups of his horse, they mistook this formal deference for real submission. To the simple Muscovites, the Tatar was the "cudgel of God," and only the sacred person of the grand prince could assuage the Lord's wrath.

The hopes and the trust of his people rested heavily on the weak shoulders of the boy. How could he lead them, he who was so devoid of power? The only act he knew how to perform was a pious one, and so he threw himself at God's mercy. He spent hours in the gloomy cathedrals lit by the flickering lights of numerous golden oil lamps. Before the shadowy icons he prostrated himself, and his forehead hit the cold stone so hard that it was discolored with bruises. There, at the steps leading to the high altar, he unburdened his troubled mind: "We have neither father nor mother nor power to reason nor strength in our fingers, but the country demands that we save it."

No answer came. If only he were older. If only he knew more or had advisers in whom he could put full trust. But coldly and silently the saints in their golden halos stared back at him. The only task he could set for himself was to survive.

His relatives urged the ten-year-old grand prince to flee the city, but he insisted on staying. The Tatars came, but they did not attack the fortified settlement itself. Having killed, looted, collected all desirable women and pressed the sturdy peasant sons into their own military service, they withdrew. Long-drawn-out sieges were not to their taste.

For the present year, the danger was over. But there would be another year, and then another. No doubt remained in anyone's mind that the Tatars meant to return.

3

CZAR of all RUSSIANS

The guards along the walls, the grand prince high up on the dais, the noblemen shouting, shoving and threatening each other with mayhem and murder—it had all happened before.

The Duma of Boyars was in session again, and Moscow's leading aristocracy were behaving in their customary fashion. But the princes and dukes had overlooked one crucial change. The grand prince was no longer an infant. Now thirteen years old, Ivan had grown into a tall, lanky youth with the sallow skin of beginning puberty. His deep-set eyes burned darkly in their sockets, making people shrink back to avoid their glare. A beaked nose and high forehead gave his face a masklike quality.

As usual, the boyars convened with a quick and rather sloppy gesture of obeisance toward the sovereign. Then they turned their backs on him and launched into their quarrels, completely forgetting his presence, as if he were some sort of inanimate object.

Ivan sat in silence. His intent mind left the present scene and recreated a picture which had been formed by his long hours of study: the glory of the Byzantine throne standing in the golden palace of Constantinople. The image dimmed and was replaced by another: the yurt of the Tatar khan, the despot sitting in cold disdain while Russian boyars, the fathers of those present, groveled before him with words and gestures of practiced self-humiliation.

The shouting grew louder. The daydreaming youth was yanked back into the grim reality.

As usual, Prince Andrei, the arrogant head of the powerful Shuisky clan, held center stage. His target was Father Sylvester, Ivan's trusted adviser.

"You better show the proper respect for your betters, lowborn priest, or you will end up as have others before you who got in the way of the Shuiskys. Remember that you came from nowhere and that you are a nobody."

The priest shrank back until he stood at the foot of the grand prince's chair. Mustering up all his courage, he spoke with quiet dignity: "My voice is the voice of the Almighty, whose cross I carry on my breast, and what I have to say is the will of our sovereign, who has honored me with his confidence."

"Sovereign, bah." Insolently Shuisky pushed the priest's chest so that he stumbled and had to hold on to the leg of the chair. Laughing uproariously, the nobleman turned to the assembly. "My fathers were princes and heroes in battle when this little boy's ancestors still collected firewood under the trees. You better listen to me if you know what is good for you. I will . . ."

"Silence, you blasphemous dog." The breaking voice from the dais pierced the general hubbub like a gunshot. The nobles froze in their boots. His mouth gaping, the surprised Shuisky turned around.

Ivan had risen. His trembling finger pointed straight at the boisterous prince. For some moments nothing moved. His cheeks were burning, and his breath came in quick spurts. Finally he controlled himself. The extended finger ceased to tremble.

"You have insulted the majesty of my house once too often, Shuisky. I may be young, but I am your master to whom you have sworn fealty."

He looked around, sweeping the chamber with his thin arm. Each man felt the eyes burning into his own. "Let no one forget it. Shuisky has desecrated the cross which he kissed in a holy oath. He stands as an offender against God and against his sovereign."

Still nobody moved. They stood frozen like the icicles which hung outside from the arched doorways.

"Guards," rang out again the voice of the enraged youth, "take this man and punish him."

Life came into the rigid row of armed men ranged against the walls of the chamber. Heavy boots stomped the stone floor. In an instant the proud prince was cowering on the floor in a crumpled heap. From their belts the guards grasped the dreaded knouts, stout parchment whips with three tails. The whips whistled through the air, cutting deeply into human flesh. The stones turned crimson. In horror the boyars retreated, trying to shrink into the tapestry-covered walls.

"Enough." The grand prince's voice was now calm and controlled. "Take this dog and throw him where he belongs: into the kennel with the other dogs."

They dragged him away. The stunned members of the Duma knew what this meant. The hunting hounds were savage and bloodthirsty. What an end for one who had wanted to reach so high.

Nobody knew whether Ivan had planned this scene or whether he acted on impulse. It was a dangerous gamble, and he had won. At the critical moment, traditional authority prevailed. Like undisciplined children the boyars had acted up when the teacher was out of the room, but habituated to obey instantly when the Tatar conquerors commanded, they now submitted without a murmur of protest. The master had finally swung the whip, and they flinched like the fierce dogs in the kennel outside which were now feasting on human flesh.

From then on, the indignities ceased. Ivan came and went, and nobody dared to bar his way. The court learned to tremble before his sudden fits of temper. Conditioned by early experience, he was constantly suspicious. He became obsessed with fears of conspiracy, with the necessity to enforce strict obedience and proper respect.

Not long after the showdown with Andrei Shuisky, a boyar addressed Ivan with too much familiarity. The guards seized him and cut out his tongue so that he would not be tempted to commit the offense a second time.

Now the grand prince freely selected his companions from among the sons of court officials and servants. At his command, they mounted spirited horses to accompany him on his rounds of amusements. The Kremlin gate opened. Down came the wooden drawbridge which spanned the water-filled moat, and the little cavalcade thundered across. In front of the ruler's horse ran his personal servant, Alexei Adashev. Moving his spindly legs at top speed, he swung his staff and cried, "Make way for the Grand Prince. Clear the road." Only when the riders had reached the outskirts could he fall back gasping for breath.

Ducks and geese, quacking in loud protest, beat a hasty retreat before the hoofs, as did pigs and goats, together with their owners. The streets of Moscow were no more than crooked alleys, frozen hard in winter and muddy, with stagnant puddles in the spring. On summer days, the horsemen raised clouds of dust which hovered over man and beast long after their passing.

The wooden houses, the many tiny churches and the outer belt of vegetable gardens were soon left behind. The young men un-slung their bows as they rode into the forest. From the Tatars they had picked up the art of shooting from the backs of their galloping mounts. Game was plentiful, from nervously zigzagging rabbits to lumbering bears. The big brown beasts were dangerous predators which brazenly entered peasant huts when severe winters made food scarce.

Away from the court, with its cumbersome formalities, the youths mingled easily and comfortably with the common people. After the hunt, they sang and swapped stories in the village taverns. On summer evenings they joined the peasants on the greens and listened as strolling singers told of the legendary and real heroes to the accompaniment of the tamboura, a lutelike folk instrument. Jugglers performed their tricks, and actors were rewarded with copper coins and with loud laughter for their satirical, bawdy farces. The church strongly condemned all such amusements, but could not suppress them. The people dutifully attended church, listened to the admonitions of the clergy and then proceeded to do as they had done before. This was as true for the simple peasant as it was for the grand prince who enjoyed the coarsest ribaldry, yet never let it interfere with his endless daily devotions.

As Ivan exchanged jokes and shared drinks with the humblest of his subjects in a rough, informal comradery, he learned much about the people he was destined to rule.

Russia was a land of sturdy, hard-working peasants. The black soil was rich and loamy. Abundant crops could easily be raised unless human greed or mismanagement interfered. Enough rye, cabbages, cucumbers, beets and onions were harvested in peaceful years to last through the long winter. Game and fish were not hard to obtain, and as for recreation, the cheapest form was to get drunk on the fermented juices of various fruits.

Still misery and hunger appeared often in the wake of raiding or war parties living off the peasant's provisions. They trampled the growing crops and burned what they could not carry away.

Even without interference by human predators, life was hard and working hours long. Water was drawn from wells with the help of long poles acting as levers. Women carried it to the house, two buckets at a time, fastened to a yoke resting on their shoulders. More prosperous peasants could afford a flat cart, drawn by a horse whose wooden harness was shaped like a wishbone.

Few peasants owned their own land. Usually it belonged to some nobleman, but he generally left the plowman to his own devices as long as part of the produce was turned over as rent. At times, peasant sons were drafted as forced laborers on the land-lord's mansion or for his military ventures. Otherwise, the village community, the *mir*, handled its own affairs in an informal demo-cratic fashion.

In each *mir*, the council of family elders assigned to every single family several strips of land so that all peasants had roughly the same opportunity to till good or poor farmland. Through its headman, the *mir* was collectively responsible for the payment of taxes. In some respects, the present collective farm setup in the Soviet Union continues the traditions of the *mir*.

Even though the peasant in Western and Central Europe had long been reduced to a state of serfdom ranking only one notch above slavery in human degradation, in the years when Ivan grew into manhood, servitude was still the exception rather than the rule in Russia.

When times were bad or the landlord unduly demanding, the family could always pack up and move on. The available space was endless, and the pioneer spirit was strong. In small groups they penetrated the spruce forest to clear patches for their fields. From the abundant timber, log cabins were built, and the grass-land furnished the raw material for the thatched roofs. This is how the Russian nation grew, as later the American nation was to grow; spreading outposts, at first isolated, were gradually forged into a mighty country.

On his outings Ivan also rubbed elbows with another important element of the Russian people, the traders. They had very little in common with the merchant princes who, at the same time, built their opulent palaces in Venice and Amsterdam and patronized the greatest among the artists and scholars. The

Russian trader knew nothing of art and scholarship; he was not even acquainted with the techniques of bookkeeping or banking. In fact, he was as illiterate as the peasant, yet he possessed cunning and courage.

In convoys of barges, the traders traveled the Volga and the other rivers in summertime, and in winter their caravans moved by sleigh and packhorse, always accompanied by armed escorts. In such places as the ancient caravan city of Samarkand, they made contacts with the merchants of Persia and even distant China, the legendary Cathay, where the streets were said to be paved with gold.

Ivan wanted to learn as much as possible about his subjects. He looked for advisers among the people he felt he could trust. Soon Adashev was relieved of running in front of the snorting horses. His first promotion was to the position of master of the royal bed-chamber. Officially this involved only making the grand prince's bed, but it brought him into close daily contact with his lord. Proving himself a calm and dependable servant, he gradually worked himself into the role of a trusted adviser. But because of his lowly beginning, Ivan was later to speak of him as "that man whom I raised from a dunghill."

While the Czar roamed the countryside, Adashev, the handy-man, and Sylvester, the priest, took over more and more of the actual government business. The boyars were thoroughly disgusted that men of such lowly birth were given such far-reaching responsibilities. But the highborn nobles only muttered their protests among themselves when the prince was out of earshot. They vividly remembered the fate of Andrei Shuisky.

On their outings, the youthful riders were not always well behaved. With Russians of all classes they shared affinity for strong drink. When they were in their cups, brawls and violence frequently resulted. Unmindful of the crowds, they galloped through the streets, trampling men, women and children under the sharp hoofs of their horses. Their forays left trails of over-

turned merchant's stalls and scattered wares. Women were insulted and men were beaten with whips for diversion. Whatever
struck the fancy of the revelers, they took without asking or
paying.

Many a time, when Ivan returned from such roistering, Father
Sylvester berated him. Fearless as an Old Testament prophet
confronting a king or high priest, he reminded Ivan that the
wrath of God strikes all evildoers, be they princes or beggars.
His voice burning with mystic fire, he told a trembling Ivan of
visions, of miraculous signs forecasting dire punishment for all
those youthful transgressions.

"Is this the example you are setting for your people?" he
thundered. "They look up to you for guidance, and you are betraying their trust. Repent, cleanse yourself."

Ivan did not call the guards. Unlike other monarchs, who considered themselves to be above moral law, he broke down in deep
remorse. "Yes, I have sinned," he cried. "I have disgraced myself.
I am lost, I am damned." The wild youth turned into a humble
penitent, and for days he would perform debasing acts of contrition, fasting, staying awake nights and praying in order to
obtain forgiveness.

His character was one of sharp contrasts. Anger and destructive
violence could abruptly give way to the bitterest self-accusation,
and he did not hesitate to shout out loudly the confessions of his
wrongdoings. The monarch recited his sins in public, for all the
court, even for all the people, to hear. But when the mood of
penance had passed, the other ego, the reckless and cruel, took
over once more.

The youthful joyrides and pranks did not interfere with the
grand prince's studies. Neither Metropolitan Macary nor Father
Sylvester needed to prompt their pupil. His eagerness to learn
was unbounded; the limits of his education were set by the
scarcity of books, not by the industry of the student.

Deeply imprinted on his mind was the concept of the autocrat, as it was often referred to in the old documents. The autocrat was the exalted Byzantine monarch, unrestricted, at least in theory, in his power over any and all his subjects.

Another title also cropped up in his readings, especially in those dealing with events closer to home. Various Tatar khans had referred to themselves as czars. His own grandfather, Ivan III, had, on occasion, signed state papers as "Czar Ivan." The word was derived from the Latin *Caesar*. Julius Caesar had been the first in a long line of all-powerful Roman chiefs of state, emperor in all but name. To honor their great precursor, all subsequent Roman monarchs had adopted his name and made "Caesar" into a title. They called themselves Caesar Augustus, Caesar Nero or Caesar Vespasianus. Now young Ivan Vasilevich tried it out as he stood alone by his high reading desk: "Caesar Ivan," "Czar Ivan." It sounded good, very good.

He was now fully grown, taller than most men he encountered. The awkward beginning of an auburn beard was sprouting on chin and cheeks. Soon it would be long and full, as every Russian wanted his beard to be. To appear clean-shaven was thought of as unmanly. Moreover, the church forbade it, with the argument that a beardless man's face resembled too much that of a woman. Such a sight might provoke in other men the lusts of perverted sexuality.

Searching one day among the papers of his late father, Ivan came upon a letter written by the monk Philoteus:

All Christian empires are fallen, and in their stead stands alone the empire of our ruler in accordance with the prophetic books. Two Romes have fallen, but the third stands, and a fourth there will not be. . . .

Here it was again, the grandiose vision of the Third Rome, the dream he had been dreaming lately more and more often.

The Third Rome had to become reality now, in his time, and any Rome, whether first, second or third, had to have a Caesar.

He sent for the Metropolitan.

"Your Excellency. I am now sixteen. It is time that I be crowned."

The prelate was stunned. "Crowned? With what? There is no crown in Moscow. None of your ancestors were crowned. They just inherited the title of grand prince. That was all. It is not a Muscovite custom."

"Then we will make it a custom, and we will find a crown, a crown which graced the emperors of Constantinople. They were crowned by the patriarch; I want to be crowned by you, Macary, not as grand prince of Moscow, but as Czar of all Russia."

The old churchman fell into deep thought. Soon he left the prince and meditated in solitude upon all the implications of his pupil's soaring ideas. The next day they spoke about it again. The more they pursued all the facets, the more Macary liked the proposition. Czar of all Russians: the boy had a vivid imagination, but the vision could become a resplendent reality, with glory for the monarch and power for the church.

Moscow was a Christian state. The now familiar notion of separation of church and state was unknown then. Eastern Orthodoxy, the faith of Moscow, could become the faith of a vast united Russia if cross and crown were united in purpose and in action. Prince and prelate were allies in this holy cause, as Macary perceived it. He, the spiritual head, would bestow the crown on the temporal head and thereby make him the sword, the executor of God's will. This would bring an end to the tragic conditions in the Russian lands. Now the people were hopelessly divided, split into many independent and semi-independent principalities, duchies and city-states, fighting among themselves, exhausting their strength by spilling the blood of fellow-Christians, of fellow–Orthodox Christians at that. All this could be overcome by a determined ruler backed by a strong church.

Yes, he, Macary, Metropolitan of Moscow and Primate of all Russian clergy, was ready to invest the young prince with the divine mission. He would drape over his shoulders the mantle that had fallen from the autocrats of Byzantium.

Drummers went out through the streets of the city, and a proclamation was read announcing the great event. It was greeted with general jubilation. This was something that struck a loud echo in the heart of every Muscovite. After all the years of weakness and confusion, there was in the air a promise of stability, a hope for new strength and for pride and glory. Strong leadership, blessed and supported by men of God: that sounded just like what was needed.

The spectacle unfolded on January 16, 1546, with all the pageantry of the Eastern Church. It was an extravaganza in which Roman symbolism blended with Byzantine magnificence and with Slavic warmth and ardor.

The people streamed to Red Square, which took on the appearance of a giant fairground. The carcasses of boars and oxen were roasting over open fires. Strong drink flowed freely from stout casks. The sound of singing and the stomping of dancing feet filled the crisp winter air. Good-naturedly the men jostled each other for a better view of the leading players in the unfolding drama.

Slowly the procession made its way across the square. The young prince cut a splendid figure on a white horse. From the saddle of richly tooled red leather hung countless little silver bells. Walking beside the horse, the highest nobles of the realm guided it by the bridle.

Ivan waved happily to the cheering crowd which poured out to him its trust and love. This was the happiest moment he had ever experienced. Solemnly the clerics carrying crosses and icons, the nobles in their finery and the delegations from many towns moved through the gate onto the Kremlin grounds to enter the Uspensky Cathedral, which was dedicated to the Virgin Mother's assumption.

Inside, hundreds of candles illuminated the multicolored

frescoes which covered the walls and the vaulted ceiling. Unable
to express their devotion through the written word, monk artists
had developed to heights of excellence this style of portraying
the greater glory of God.

Compared with the famed basilicas in Constantinople or in
Rome, this cathedral was small, though it rated as Moscow's
foremost place of worship. Eastern Orthodox sanctuaries were
not meant to hold huge assemblages of worshipers at one time.
The services extended over many hours, and so people usually
drifted in, stayed for a while and left again to make room for
others. While inside they watched the solemn proceedings, kissed
the icons and frequently made the sign of the cross.

The high point of the liturgy, when the bread and the wine,
blessed by the priest, turned miraculously into the body and the
blood of Christ occurred hidden from common eyes, behind the
iconostasis, a screen richly painted with numerous icons. Only
after the mystery was completed did clergy and accolytes issue
forth from behind the screen to offer the consecrated eucharist
to the faithful while the male chorus announced the joyous event
with a hymn of glorification.

This time the cathedral remained packed throughout the whole
service. The crowd extended through the open doors and filled
all the spaces on the Kremlin grounds. The chants seemed to
come from the opened heavens themselves, so powerful sounded
the massed voices of the monks, who had come from monasteries
far and wide.

When the last chorus of "God, have mercy on us" had waned,
when the celebrating priest had, for the last time, blessed the
worshipers with the two lighted tapers in each hand, a deep calm
settled over the assemblage. In the midst of silent anticipation,
the grand prince rose from his knees. Sylvester and Adashev, his
chief advisers, stepped to his side and conducted him to a throne
which had been placed in front of the now hidden high altar.
The throne was hand-carved of rare woods, the work of the best

craftsmen in the land. Legs, armrests and back were richly inlaid with plated gold.

As Ivan approached the throne, he prostrated himself before every icon along his way. Only then did he seat himself.

For the occasion, the chests which his grandfather's Greek wife had once brought with her from beleaguered Constantinople had been opened to yield the royal regalia she had been able to salvage. Ivan wore the mantle, the heavy collar of pearls and the diamond-studded belt which the Byzantine emperors had once used.

All twenty-one bells of the cathedral burst into a crescendo as Metropolitan Macary approached the throne. From a velvet pillow he took a pointed golden hat alive with the sparkle of a hundred diamonds. A brim of rich shiny fur encircled this tall headgear, the crown once worn by Constantine Monomach, Emperor of Eastern Rome. Ivan IV was the first of a long line of Russian Czars to be crowned with the golden crown of Monomach.

The bells continued their unmelodious metallic clangor as the Metropolitan anointed the prince's forehead with consecrated oil. Then the crown was placed on his bowed head. A golden cross-shaped scepter, studded with precious stones blessed by the prelate, was extended into the young monarch's right hand.

"Ivan Vasilevich," intoned Macary, "son of many glorious princes of Moscow, a new day is dawning for this your faithful city which you will make the head of a mighty empire. In the name of the Holy Trinity and of all the saints and with the consent of the honorable boyars and of all the people, I hereby crown you Czar of all Russia."

A thunderous cheer went up toward the cathedral lofts, sustained as if it would never end. It rolled on into the Kremlin grounds and from there through the open gates to where the masses in the square picked it up until all Moscow seemed to ring with the raucous roar of jubilation. For a day, happiness reigned unchecked in this frontier town, which was overcome with a sense of destiny—the destiny to become a great world power.

The new Czar left the cathedral. Velvet and damask cloth had been spread on the ground for his feet to tread on. The nobles showered him with handfuls of small gold coins. Ahead of the guard detachment strode the standard-bearer, who carried the new Russian emblem, the double-headed eagle, once the standard of Byzantium. The eagle had come from Rome to Constantinople, and now it came to Moscow to roost.

Ivan walked between the rows of his warriors, drawn up in gala review. Old men, infirm with the wounds of many battles, bent their knees and cast their eyes downward so as not to offend the czar's majesty, so newly endowed with divine authority.

As soon as the Czar had returned to his palace, the common people were allowed to enter the Kremlin grounds, just for this unique occasion. Children and adults scrambled in the snow for the coins scattered during the procession. When none were left, the crowd tore up the cloth. They stormed into the cathedral itself to strip the throne and seats of the notables of their hangings. Any shred that had been used in the solemn ceremony was carried away as a souvenir and as a potent charm to bring luck and to ward off evil in the days and years to come.

4

THE BRIDE

One topic of conversation overshadowed all others in Moscow's social circles: who would become the Czar's bride?

Ivan wanted to marry, and even if it had not been his wish, reasons of state made that step urgent. He was still an adolescent, but anybody's life, old or young, could be snuffed out in a moment. Aside from poison and assassination, which were ever-present threats to the existence of a high personage, medical science was still in its infancy. Killing disease struck without warning in palace and hovel alike.

It was urgent that an heir to the throne be born at the earliest possible moment. At Grand Prince Vasili's death, it was bad enough that the successor was a small child. How infinitely worse would it have been had the ruler died childless. The resulting confusion could have lasted for generations.

The guessing game was on. Would the young Czar follow his grandfather's example and court a foreign princess? Political marriages for the purpose of cementing alliances were quite common among crowned heads. Or would he choose a mate from among the top-ranking families which only so recently had contested his position? The heads of the Shuiskys, the Bielskys and the other leading clans saw themselves already in the role of in-laws to the monarch. In this way, old wounds could be patched up and enemies turned into friends.

One situation, so common in our own society, was completely out of the question: that Ivan would by chance meet a girl somewhere and that they would fall in love and decide to share their lives from then on.

Marrying for love was not in the cards for wearers of a crown anywhere, and in Russia it was not done at all, at any social level. Matches were arranged by the parents. Even when occasionally the prospective groom had some voice in the matter, the girl almost never did.

Women were treated as an inferior species, just a step above horses and cattle. The Mongol invasion had brought in its wake a strong oriental influence. Upon their conversion to Islam, the Tatars secluded their women, especially after they were married, so that no roving male eye could rest upon them. Imitating their overlords of the steppe, the Russian nobility likewise confined their wives to the *terem,* their version of the oriental harem.

Waited on by numerous servant maids, the noblewomen spent their days in enforced idleness, which was especially deadening since they were almost uniformly illiterate and ignorant of any pursuits of the mind. Even the rearing of children was turned over to serving women, so needlework and gossip remained as the only diversions.

Women rarely ventured out of their houses. Prayers were said in the chapels attached to their homes. On the infrequent occasions when they did leave their gilded prisons, they rode in closed and curtained carriages or were carried in litters by bearers who hardly knew what their mistresses looked like since they were invariably deeply veiled when away from their homes.

Odd as it may seem, the women of the lower classes enjoyed a far greater measure of freedom. The market wife or the peasant woman could hardly be secluded since she had to work. So being a woman meant either long days of hard labor in field or marketplace or endless hours of boredom in the company of equally bored aunts, sisters or ladies-in-waiting.

No wonder that, despite all precautions, the ladies occasionally sought excitement in extramarital adventures. When a husband discovered the misdeed, he was apt to pack the errant wife off to a convent for the rest of her days. This also happened when he simply wanted to get rid of her.

Nevertheless, among all social classes weddings were big events which often extended over several days given to music, dancing and heavy drinking. In the religious ceremony the future role of the wife was clearly laid out when the priest intoned, "As the holy cross is the head of the church, so the husband is the head of his wife."

At peasant weddings it was customary that the groom's father give his son a whip as a gift. The bride knelt before her new master, and he playfully struck her across the shoulder. As the years of married life rolled by, he was likely to use this instrument more forcefully on his mate, who came to expect this sort of periodic attention.

A German tradesman, one of the many who had come to live in Moscow, had taken a Russian wife. After some time, she complained that he did not love her. "How so?" he inquired. "Don't I provide for you? Don't you have cloaks to wear and jewelry to adorn yourself?"

"True," answered the woman. "You provide for me well, but during our whole marriage you have not beaten me a single time."

A man who beat his wife was at least a husband who noticed her. The German promised to mend his ways.

We should remember that women living in western countries were, on the whole, not much better off, but an etiquette of gallantry made their lot at least appear better on the surface. There existed an ideal of love and courtship, though it lived mainly in the songs of the troubadours and, more recently, in the printed stories about famous lovers. But Russia had no troubadours. Nobody serenaded his lady love by moonlight under her window. Romeo and Juliet had no Muscovite counterparts, nor did writers bother with romances like the tale of Tristan and Isolde.

Ivan knew nothing about the refined ways of courting, and even had he known, he would hardly have introduced them into his empire. But being the avid reader that he was, he had in one of the chronicles come upon an old Russian custom which attracted him. He immediately decided to revive it.

Messengers hurriedly spread through the city, and on the next morning the nobility assembled in the Cathedral of the Assumption to hear an important announcement.

Tension was in the air, and even during divine services—which, as always, preceded the proclamation—the subdued buzzing of voices was not completely silenced. At long last, the Czar rose, and after invoking the blessings of all the saints, he declared:

Putting my trust in God and His Immaculate Mother, I have thought to marry. I had at first intended to seek marriage in a foreign court, but I have now foregone that intention because I was orphaned and left a small child after the death of my father and my mother. And if I take a wife in a foreign country and afterwards we do not get on well together, it will be difficult for us. Therefore I wish to marry within my own country the one whom God will bless to be my wife.

Ivan paused. He was a superb public speaker, and his timing was excellent. The audience sat taut and expectant. It was obvious that the listeners approved of what they had heard so far. But the crucial moment was now to come. Who would it be? Which family would be raised up to sit next to the throne?

The Czar continued, and his words fell upon utterly amazed ears. The tension dissolved in disappointment. A scheme was unveiled which nobody had expected, which came as a stunning surprise.

The *voevodes* (district governors) were given orders to round up all virgins of noble birth in their districts and to convey them to the capital. Fathers, even of the lowest aristocratic echelon, were forbidden to hide their eligible daughters under threat of severe punishment.

It was a beauty contest with the prize being not a movie contract or a college scholarship, but the hand of God's chosen ruler and the title of Czarina. Two thousand strong, the flower of Russian womanhood converged on Moscow. While the high aristocracy nursed its disappointment, the common people enjoyed themselves watching carriage upon carriage drive up to the Kremlin gates and disgorge beauties from all corners of the realm. The whole affair had a kind of democratic flavor, since the selection had not been restricted to the top families. Besides, there was anticipation in the air similar to that prevailing just before a major sports event in our own days.

Physicians and midwives circulated among the candidates to screen out those of poor health and others who seemed too frail for the all-important task of childbearing. A slim figure was cause enough for elimination, for the Russian taste in female beauty ran towards plumpness.

The day of the contest dawned. Only one hundred girls had survived the screening. Their maids helped them into the many layers of clothing which modest Russian women were accustomed to wearing. The outermost garment was a loose gown reaching to the ground, white or scarlet, with wide loose sleeves and large gold buttons. Modesty also demanded that the hair always be covered; therefore a cape of rich fur was draped over head and shoulders. No belt or girdle encircled the waist, for it was thought to be unseemly to reveal the contours of the human body. Boots of leather embroidered with pearls, bracelets and crosses of rubies worn as pendants completed the outfit.

The ordeal of preparation continued through the application of heavy make-up, which was then the high fashion. Poor complexions were hidden under thick powder, and defective teeth did not show up because both uppers and lowers were stained black as coal.

When the contestants finally lined up for the crucial inspection, most of them felt faint. Surrounded by clerks and guards, the Czar made his entrance. He proceeded slowly, stopping and moving on again, measuring and appraising like a careful shopper who is about to make a costly purchase.

He took his time, and the girls shivered under their voluminous raiments. At long last, Ivan halted in front of a girl who was strikingly different from the others. Among the generally ample figures, hers stood out, tall and slender. Somehow her lack of weight had escaped the scrutiny of the midwives. Her hair was bluish black, and her skin had a natural pale sheen.

A slight wave of the royal hand alerted an attendant. Ivan took from him a silken handkerchief and dropped it into the lap of the deeply curtseying Anastasia Zakharin-Romanov. She was the daughter of a deceased minor nobleman of Prussian origin, but her family had the advantage of never having been involved in the wrangling for power during Ivan's childhood.

So entered the name of Romanov, then unknown to anybody except a few neighbors, into history. Nobody else had ever heard it, and nobody anticipated that it would be the name of a long line of czars. The last czar of Russia, the one who lost his life in the Bolshevik Revolution of 1917, was a Romanov.

Whatever the misgivings of the leading clans, the choice was made. On the same evening the bethrothal was celebrated at a rousing banquet. Of course, only the men participated. The guests ate rare meats from golden plates and drank toast after toast of Hungarian wine to the young pair's health. Though the setting was one of extreme luxury, no silverware was provided because every man customarily carried his own knife and spoon dangling from his belt.

At the height of the merrymaking, the women made their entrance. Led by Anna Glinsky, the Czar's only surviving grandmother, and followed by her ladies-in-waiting, Anastasia descended the stairway into the big hall, holding a large golden goblet. The heads of the princely houses approached, and as she offered them the cup to sip, they delicately kissed her cheek or forehead. The ceremony over, the ladies retired, and the party continued until most of the guests had to be helped to their quarters by their grooms.

Ivan and Anastasia were married less than a month after the coronation. Following the lengthy religious rites, the couple were ceremonially conducted to their chamber, where they mounted the wedding couch under the watchful eyes of the highest dignitaries.

Then came the honeymoon. Time-honored custom and the Czar's special inclination made it not a pleasure trip but a strenuous pilgrimage. In penitent's clothing they walked through the snow to the Troitsko (Trinity) Monastery near the capital, where, for several days, they prayed at the grave of St. Sergei, Russia's favorite miracle-working saint. From Troitsko they continued by sleigh to other abbeys and shrines farther away.

Throughout his life, Ivan undertook such pilgrimages, irrespective of weather and unconcerned about the welfare of those who had to accompany him. At times the itinerary led far to the north, into the frozen world of the Arctic. As long as she could, Anastasia followed her husband on all his voyages. Her delicate health suffered, but she never complained whether their barge was buffeted by strong river currents or their carriage bumped over roads which were no more than ruts beaten into the grass by wagonwheels. Once, to reach an isolated monastery on the coast of Murmansk, they even had to mount reindeer.

As soon as he was ensconced inside a monastery, the Czar faithfully attended the endless daily services. It was among the monks that the impressive liturgy of the Orthodox Church flowered in its richest colors.

Ivan also loved to hold long disputations with individual monks who had gained wide fame for their saintliness. He argued with them fine points of theology and even consulted them on state policy. At these times imperial pride was laid aside, and frank, even highly critical counsel was encouraged.

The monasteries formed a skeleton around which arose the Russian civilization. Small bands of black-robed monks fled from the noise of battle or escaped from the sinful ways of the towns into the green wilderness. Far from other habitations, they felled trees to build their log chapels. The long days were divided between hard labor and religious devotions. Missionary work was carried on among the pagan Finns and Laps.

In time, fugitive peasants joined the monks and relieved them of the manual chores. More land was cleared. Many monasteries acquired large holdings which brought wealth into the coffers of the once poor penitents. The Troitsko Monastery alone employed over a thousand workers. While some monks continued in their saintly ways, others gave themselves to the temptations of luxury. Even gross immorality found its way into these nearly self-contained communities.

Whatever cultural life existed among the Russian people was nurtured largely inside the fortified monastery walls. There the powerfully haunting chants of the liturgy were perfected, icons painted and ancient scrolls copied. Compared with some of their Catholic counterparts, the eastern monks remained, for the most part, concerned primarily with their traditional faith. A visiting bishop commented to Pope Clement VII on the almost complete absence of classical learning. "Russians," he reported, "have no knowledge of philosophy, astronomy, speculative physics or other liberal sciences."

The Orthodox monks made up for their shortcomings in accomplishments of the mind by their most generous charity. Large numbers of the poor were fed in times of need. The Czar and other persons of rank were not above taking advantage of monastic hospitality by inviting themselves and their large retinues for prolonged visits. Perhaps to compensate for such freeloading and also to pay their way out of divine wrath for their wrongdoings, the wealthy frequently made over large tracts of land to the monks.

The monasteries occupied a large place in the life of the average Russian. They sheltered numerous relics, and these relics were credited with the power to heal, to bring fortune, to ward off evil. People still harbored many pagan ideas which were only thinly covered by a layer of Christian piety. So the good churchgoers found it not incongruous to surround the relics with gifts. They also called in monks from the nearest monastery to exorcise evil spirits which they blamed for physical or mental illness, for childlessness and even for the sickness of the cattle.

On the whole, the Russian monk was a kindly soul, but conservative to the bone. He abhorred any change in ritual or in the ways of life, and he condemned all worldly pleasures, though at times he yielded to them when tempted by the growing wealth of his religious community.

On the drawn-out pilgrimages and back home in their palace, Ivan and Anastasia spent much time together. Something happened which hardly anybody, least of all Ivan himself, had expected: he fell in love with his wife. From the casual and very one-sided selection based only on looks blossomed a deep, abiding affection. This was something rare indeed, given the social customs of Russian society at the time.

In his turbulent life, the Czar was to associate with many women, but Anastasia was the only one he ever loved. Their characters complemented each other beautifully. While he was

impulsive, as if driven by demons, and while his violent out-
breaks were followed by long periods of lonely brooding, his
mate displayed equanimity and patience. She was gentle and
retiring. With her Ivan's tortured mind could always find rest
and tranquillity. When he called her "my little heifer," it was
a name of endearment, strange as it may sound to foreign ears.
The years of young married love turned out to be the only
happy ones in the life of Czar Ivan IV.

5

IVAN the GOOD

Pilgrimages and marital bliss left the young Czar little time to attend to the business of government. It remained largely in the hands of his trusted aides, Sylvester and Adashev, who shared with the Boyar Council the burden of decision-making.

More and more power slipped into the hands of the Glinsky family, Ivan's relatives on his late mother's side. Their cruelty and blatant selfishness made them extremely unpopular. There was much grumbling about corruption and neglect, but never in the Czar's presence. Any failure to show him the abject submission which he expected as his due could bring about one of his dreaded fits of rage, and woe to the clerk or courtier who got in his way. Corporal punishment, dished out by the exalted hand of the monarch himself, was the usual penalty.

A mild June day in 1547 found the royal couple resting in the village of Ostrovka after its latest excursion. They stayed at a spacious country house overlooking the village's only street, alive with fowl and piglets rooting in the mud. It was a quiet morning. Ivan felt relaxed, his restlessness and eternal suspicions forgotten for the moment in the presence of the submissive Anastasia.

A commotion in the courtyard roused them from their leisurely

midday repast. Through the window Ivan saw his guards arguing with a group of strangers carrying bags of presents. A telltale
frown appeared on his forehead. The smile on his lips froze.
The servants recognized the brewing storm and scampered out
of his way.

With long angry strides he stormed out of the house and confronted the visitors. "Who are you? Who called you? How dare
you intrude here?"

The ninety bearded men in fur-trimmed ankle-length coats
called caftans prostrated themselves in the mud. Then a silver-
haired merchant, obviously the leader of the callers, summoned
up all his courage. "Gracious lord, forgive us the intrusion. We
come as a delegation from Pskov, your faithful city. Our people
are greatly disturbed. They have sent us to ask your protection
from injustice."

Ivan's features turned livid. What did he care about the
worries of these peddlers in sheepskins and ropes? Why didn't
they go to the local *voevode* instead of bothering him with their
petty grievances? Subjects approach the ruler when he calls
them, not when they feel like it. This was sheer effrontery
approaching insubordination.

In vain the men from Pskov tried to tell him of their woes.
It was none other than the *voevode* they had come to complain
about. The governor extracted unreasonable taxes with the help
of imprisonment and torture. The commerce of the once wealthy
city was in danger of collapsing. Not long ago, Pskov had been
an independent city. Only grudgingly had it submitted to the
Muscovite overlords. The tradition of self-government was still
alive. They felt it was their right to lay their grievances before
the person of the ruler.

Ivan was not in the mood to listen, even less to engage in
reasonable discussion. "Bind those impertinent troublemakers,"
he shouted to the guards. "We will teach them to run to their
sovereign as if he were the local policeman."

When it came to inflicting punishment, the son of Vasili showed surprising originality and inventiveness. He had hot wine brought from the cellar. Personally he went down the rows of shaking delegates and poured the liquid over their heads and beards. At his command, the guards pushed the men down into the mud. Lighted pine torches were brought to set them on fire. The victims were giving up hope of leaving the place alive. They were murmuring their last prayers.

But this was not to be their destiny.

A rider suddenly galloped through the gate scattering the loudly protesting fowl and piglets. Before even reining in his frothing mount, the messenger gasped, "Fire. Moscow is in flames. The Kremlin is burning."

The men from Pskov were forgotten. Stables were opened, wagons dragged out, horses saddled. Within the hour, Ivan, followed by a large retinue, was off to his capital.

Moscow had seen fires before. It was a city of wooden houses, each with its big stove for cooking and heating. Charcoal constantly glowed in the numerous smithies. The merchant stalls were of pine lumber. Wooden planks formed walkways over the ice in winter and over the mud in spring.

This time the conflagration had started in a little wooden church on the outskirts. A strong gale whipped the flames into the merchant quarters. With lightning speed they spread through the streets and jumped the Moskva River and the brick ramparts of the Kremlin. There a powder magazine exploded with an infernal roar, showering debris over a wide area.

In a wild stampede people rushed to the river. Many suffocated; others were trampled to death. A groan of despair went up as they saw the great cathedral bell fall from its tower, bursting into pieces on the ground. It was a terrible omen.

Priests tried in vain to rescue icons from the burning churches. Most were lost. The venerable Metropolitan, Macary, was trapped in his residence by the flames. Through a secret passage he fled to the steep bank of the river. Monks tried to lower him to the water level by a rope, but the rope broke. The fall left him bleeding and unconscious.

There was no way to check the fire. It took several days to burn itself out. Over two thousand persons had perished. Slowly the survivors began to trickle back from the surrounding villages and monasteries where they had fled. Everywhere soot-blackened figures were digging in the debris in search for the corpses of relatives and in the hope of salvaging some of their possessions.

Where was the Czar? He was not with them. Soon after entering the burning city, he had left it again to seek refuge for himself and his wife in the countryside. He was powerfully built, but where his personal safety was involved, he possessed the heart of a coward.

Nobody blamed the Czar for his cautiousness, at least not openly. But the bereaved Muscovites needed a scapegoat. What caused the fire? They were not satisfied to explain it by natural causes. Rumors of black magic made the rounds. Somebody must have dug up a corpse, cut out the heart and soaked it in water. With that hellish brew, he had sprinkled the houses which made them burst into flames. Where superstition is a way of life, such a story sounds quite plausible, especially where a state of general hysteria exists.

The church did nothing to counteract such an explanation. In fact, it shared the general belief in spells, sorcery and amulets. And the boyars? Believing the rumor or not, they were ready to exploit it. They harbored a long-standing grudge against the powerful Glinskys. Now the occasion had come to get even with them and, since they were the Czar's relatives, to remind him that he depended on boyar support.

They called an investigation into the causes of the fire. It was not an impartial search for facts, but an emotion-laden mass meeting in Red Square, ringed by blackened ruins from which still rose foul-smelling smoke. The people were in rags which covered festering burns. Almost everybody had lost relatives.

Boyar speakers asked leading questions. Their thinly veiled hints clearly pointed at the Glinskys. Somebody screamed, "Look over there. That's one of them, Prince Yuri." The prince, an uncle of the Czar, had made the fatal mistake of mingling with the crowd.

Hot fury rose around him. "Seize him. Kill him, the murderer, the arsonist. Kill him and his mother. Kill the whole accursed Glinsky brood."

Too late the hapless prince slipped away, trying to lose himself in the labyrinthal hallways and stairways of the Kremlin. The mob, now mad with the thirst for blood, cornered him inside the Uspensky Cathedral. On consecrated ground he was lynched, and his blood splashed against the holy icons.

The first kill only whetted the appetite of the crazed mob. The hunt was on for more Glinskys and for their servants. Somebody had only to shout, "Here goes one," and a life was snuffed out. The crowd had no time to check on identities. By now the masses were hunting mainly for Princess Anna Glinsky, grandmother of the Czar. The boyars had pointed their fingers especially at her, and she had been accepted as the chief culprit.

A huge throng marched out to Vorobiovo in the Sparrow Hills where Ivan was still hiding out from the smell and the smoke of the catastrophe. He could see them come, brandishing clubs and pitchforks, shouting hoarsely, "Give us Anna Glinsky. Give us the sorceress."

He was not going to comply. Instead he called the commander of the armed men who formed his bodyguard. Swinging their axes and their knouts, the well-trained soldiers threw themselves against the marchers. The first row of the mob disintegrated. Bodies writhed on the ground. The crowd behind them fell back stunned by the unexpected show of ruthless strength. Rushing, pushing each other out of the way, they dispersed. Only the corpses of those felled by the Czar's guards remained behind.

Ivan had won the day, but what a sad victory it was. His mood was grim. Nobody dared go near him, except Sylvester, the priest. Like an angel of vengeance, he confronted his master. "The thunder of God has come upon thee, O Czar, for thy idleness and evil passions. Fire from heaven has consumed Moscow and the cup of God's wrath has been poured into the hearts of the people. Mend your ways. Live up to your mission as ruler."

Ivan's shoulders sagged in despair. He spent the whole night in the chapel, brooding, bruising his forehead on the cold stones. As the first rays of the morning sun filtered in, he came to a decision. A new era was to begin.

Historians have compared the change in Ivan's attitude with a religious conversion, such as that of Paul on the road to Damascus. Mysticism and spirituality were certainly involved to a high degree, but other motives were also at work in reshaping the old Ivan into a new personality. Always concerned with his personal safety, the Czar realized with a shudder how close he himself had come to sharing the fate of his uncle, whose body was still being displayed on Red Square like that of an executed criminal. Nobody had called for the Czar's blood, but the fury against the Glinskys could easily have been redirected against their anointed relative. The march to his country refuge was a clear protest against his lack of concern, against his failure to provide leadership when leadership was badly needed.

In long hours of counsel with Sylvester and Adashev a plan took shape to fulfill the people's desire for a strong leader, to make him master in his own house, in fact as well as in name.

Again the seventeen-year-old monarch was riding toward Moscow. But what a different journey it was. Instead of rushing to a tragedy-stricken city, he now traveled slowly surrounded by a splendid cavalcade. The news of his approach preceded him from village to village, from hut to hut. By the time he arrived within the gates of his capital, his subjects filled Red Square to the last square foot of reddish dust. They fell to their knees as he passed and crossed themselves as if the Almighty Himself had arrived in their midst.

All the anger of the last weeks was forgotten. The Little Father was back again. He had come to be with them; he had a message for them.

Ivan mounted a wooden platform. It took him only a few words to establish rapport with the mass which surged around him. It was a masterful speech, a speech in which he bared his tormented soul. The people who looked up to him as God's anointed also could identify with him as a suffering human being with weaknesses like their own.

Because of my sins, of my being an orphan, and my immaturity, many people perished in quarrels, and I grew up in neglect, without instruction, accustomed only to the low cunning of boyar practices. And since that time, how greatly have I sinned before God, and how many punishments has God sent down on us.

Many listeners were in tears, filled with deep pity for the youth who had been deprived of his childhood, and who was repenting his shortcomings with such apparent contrition. Nobody would ever know how much in this amazing speech expressed sincere feelings and how much was well-calculated strategy to produce dramatic effects.

For the Muscovites listening to their ruler, it was a miracle. He was declaring himself for the little people against the mighty lords under whose suppression they had all suffered for so long. Surely a new day was breaking.

"God bless you, Little Father," they shouted as he paused for a brief moment.

Goodly people, given into our care by God, I invoke your faith in Him and your love for me. Be forgiven, I can only save you from future oppression and extortion. Forget what has happened; it will not happen again. Put enmity and hate from you. Let us all join in Christian love. Henceforth I will be your judge and your defender.

They went back to their houses in a daze. Their hopes had been raised to a pinnacle, and they were sustained during the following months as they saw their Czar plunge with all his energy into the task of ruling, which he had so long left to others.

Orders went out to rebuild the city bigger and better than ever before. Soon endless wagon trains with building materials rumbled through the outskirts. The forges of the nailmakers were ablaze day and night. Timber was plentiful, and the Muscovites knew well how to swing an ax. Ivan called in Italian architects, German masons and Danish silversmiths to repair the Kremlin structures, and he paid them generously from the treasure chests hidden below the palace. The air was filled with the clanging of hammers and the smell of freshly cut wood, and also with eagerness and optimism.

Ivan was now the most popular man in Russia, for it soon became evident that there was much more on his mind than the rebuilding of fire-charred walls. He had set himself the gigantic task of transforming the Russian state from a name into a reality.

The vast territory over which his nominal rule extended could then hardly be called a state. Between isolated towns and settlements lay vast stretches of no-man's-land held by hostile forces. The frontiers were ill defined and were frequently breached by raiding nomads.

The number-one obstacle to the Czar's sovereignty lay in the power of the various Russian princes, nominally subject to his command but still wielding nearly independent powers. They, in turn, commanded the loyalty of lesser nobles and combined with numerous relatives into widespread networks of interlocking clans.

Many princely households rivaled the Czar's court in lavishness. In the towns and villages of their vast domains, the high nobility collected taxes, kept their own armed forces and conducted their own private wars. They even carried on negotiations with foreign powers in defiance of Moscow. But whether united or quarreling among one another, the princes and boyars all lived off the labor of the common people.

With determination and courage Ivan IV began to attack the existing conditions. The Council of Boyars was pushed into the background. To pool brain power and to get a wide range of ideas, a large advisory group, the Chosen Council, was called together. All council members were encouraged to speak their mind, but Sylvester and Adashev remained the top counselors.

Alexei Adashev was charged with receiving petitions from anybody who had a grievance, with seeing that wrongs were righted. He was told by his master, "Relieve me of my sadness for the suffering people whom God has entrusted to me. Do not fear the powerful or famous when they behave unjustly. Investigate all plaints carefully and report the truth to me, fearing only the judge in heaven."

There was to be no more harassment of petitioners such as the men of Pskov had encountered.

Ordinances issued forth from the Kremlin in rapid succession. The people were given the right to elect their own local tax collectors. Provincial governors who heretofore ruled almost independently were brought under closer supervision and made to account for their behavior in office.

The year 1550 saw the completion of a law code to ensure uniform justice throughout the country. Up to that time, a law in force in Moscow was not always recognized in Pskov or Novgorod. Punishment depended on the whim of the noble judge. A wrong done by a nobleman to a commoner was hardly ever righted.

To govern effectively Ivan needed a body of dependable administrators. Traditionally the princes and boyars had held a monopoly on government functions, and they were unused to receiving and following orders. Officers were not distributed according to ability or training. To be a general, a judge or a governor one only needed the right family standing. Nobody would dream of accepting a mission ranking lower than what was customarily held by members of his family. This insistence on precedence extended to such trivial matters as the place in a ceremonial procession or the seating at a banquet table. At a time when the feudal system was already breaking up in the countries of Western Europe, it was still deeply entrenched east of the Alps.

Ivan was clever enough to realize that he could not dislocate the territorial lords from their privileged positions all at once. But he was determined to make a beginning.

In order to break the stranglehold of the boyars, another class of people had to be found to carry on the business of government. The Czar did not reach down to the peasantry or the traders, but he began to upgrade the lower nobility. He freed them from their accustomed role as retainers to the higher aristocracy and made them into the "serving gentry," the *pomeshchiks*. Among them were distributed army commands, diplomatic posts and positions in various government bureaus. Their responsibility was only to the Czar, who could both punish and reward them. He was determined to command the complete loyalty of this new manpower pool.

The problem of reward was a particularly difficult one. In our society it comes naturally that civil service should be rewarded with a regular income in money. But Russia's economy was still predominantly agricultural. Land was the measure of wealth, not money. And where was the Czar going to get enough land to keep the serving gentry loyal and content? This question was to be with him throughout his reign.

His own family had large holdings, but this was not enough.

Most other land was in the hands of the princes and boyars, but Ivan still felt too weak to expropriate the feudal lands. This would have meant cutting at the very roots of the dominant aristocracy. He had to wait for such a frontal attack, but he was sure that the time would come.

In his search for land to reward the faithful *pomeshchiks,* Ivan cast longing glances at the vast stretches of field and forest, nearly one third of all available land, which was not held by the nobility, but by the church—particularly by the numerous monasteries.

This put a trying burden on his conscience. Because of his extreme devotion, priests and monks were dear to his heart, and on his frequent pilgrimages he showered churches and monasteries with costly gifts. Yet it became obvious that, to be master in his realm, he could not relinquish control over such vast portions of his territory, not even to the clergy.

He hesitated to boldly oust the monks from their land as his contemporary Henry VIII of England had done. This also would have to wait for a later time. For the present, it was found necessary, as a first step, to weld the church into a uniform organization under the firm control of the crown. Ivan decided to move in this direction. To subject the church to the will of the state did not seem as hard a task as in the West, where popes had often proclaimed their supremacy over all Christians, including kings and emperors. The Eastern Orthodox Church had never made such claims.

In accord with Metropolitan Macary and with Father Sylvester, the Czar called a synod, an assembly of all bishops and abbots. They met in 1551 with the full pomp characteristic of the church. The bishops came in their golden crowns, and the archimandrites, the higher monastic superiors, wore their black miters and carried their long staffs. After divine services, attended by the whole court, the proceedings got under way. The churchmen had expected that they would merely be called upon to give their blessings to Ivan's judicial and administrative reforms, and this they were only too willing to do.

But they were in for a surprise. The Metropolitan demanded that they address themselves to a complete overhaul of the church itself. A thorough housecleaning was long overdue. Monasteries had lapsed into sexual license. Many priests were so ignorant that they could not even read the prayers. Drunkenness among the clergy was widespread.

The worthy prelates could hardly deny the truth of such accusations. Measures were taken to curb the abuses.

This was as far as the leaders of Orthodoxy would go. Any suggestions for a reexamination of the more basic religious ideas were rejected. Nothing happened that could be compared with the great theological debate which convulsed the West at that time and divided it into a Catholic and a Protestant camp. Instead the synod spent many days in heated discussion over such trivia as whether, during divine services, the sign of the cross should be made with two fingers or with three. The two-finger party won out.

But it is to the glory of Eastern Orthodoxy that it remained free from the violent effects of intolerance which blemished the Western churches. No Inquisition tortured suspected heretics, and no public bonfires roasted them to the greater exhaltation of God. In this respect Spaniards, Englishmen and Germans could have taken a lesson from the Muscovites.

The most delicate question brought before the synod and also the most important one for Ivan's designs was that of church possessions. Weren't the men of God extremely wealthy? And did such wealth not conflict with the poverty of Christ himself and his early disciples?

The assembly split right down the middle on this disturbing issue. Many, Sylvester among them, favored a return to apostolic poverty, but others argued that the church, representing the glory of heaven on earth, needed its gold and its brocaded raiments. The faithful, even though poor themselves, wanted to be impressed by the magnificence of their religion. Besides, the monasteries needed their wealth to practice charity, which they so often had occasion to do.

The aged Metropolitan sided with the latter view, and his enormous prestige helped to carry the day.

The Czar did not interfere. The time was not ripe for a radical break with tradition. He needed the goodwill of the church in his design to build a strong centralized government. But he also needed land desperately; otherwise all the progress would be halted by the inability to compensate the new corps of the serving nobility.

Without disturbing the ecclesiastical system as a whole, Ivan imposed, on his own authority, some restrictions on further land-grabbing by the church. No more donations to monasteries could be made without his approval, and some, dating back to his childhood, were declared void; the land reverted to the crown.

While his ancestors had been little more than the largest landholders in the region, Ivan IV was beginning to assume the role of an autocrat who combined Byzantine grandeur with Mongol despotism. The foundations of a unified Russia began to emerge. But the obstacles remaining in his path were still formidable. The forces of the past were deeply entrenched. If the goal was to be reached in the foreseeable future, a direct assault would eventually have to be launched against the divisive powers and privileges of prince and boyar, of bishop and monk.

6

IVAN the CONQUEROR

With calculated insolence the Tatar emissaries strode into the throne room. They did not prostrate themselves before the sacred person of the Czar, and their peaked fur caps remained stuck to their shaven skulls.

"Ivan Vasilevich," intoned their spokesman in a flat contemptuous voice which mixed Russian and Mongolian words into a brogue only barely understandable by the man addressed. "You are not a child anymore. You have grown into manhood, and my lord, Khan Saip of the Crimea, will not wait any longer. He wants to know your intentions. Do you want his brotherly love, or do you want war?"

"Is this the whole message, you cur of an infidel?" Ivan's face was showing the telltale marks of the oncoming storm. But the envoy either did not know the significance of the suddenly reddening cheeks and the light froth at the mouth or else calculatedly decided to ignore it.

"Now hear the full message, Prince of Moscow. If you want my khan's love, send him suitable presents and promise him an annual tribute of 15,000 gold pieces, as your ancestors have done. Then you will have peace."

"Have you done, son of a she dog? You will hear my answer

in due time. As for now—" he waved to the guards. In a moment the Tatars were tightly bound with ropes and dragged off to the dungeons below.

The Czar's hot anger was cooled for the moment, but that did not solve the very serious problem of the Tatars. Ivan knew it only too well: none of the internal reforms, which had got off to such an auspicious start, could have any lasting effect unless the monarchy showed strength towards the outside. Russians wanted to live behind secure frontiers. They had yet to develop a national pride, and such pride could best be infused by the clash of arms in battle against a common enemy.

Though the descendants of the Golden Horde were now split into rival khanates, often embroiled in fratricidal feuds, they were still formidable enemies. Two Tatar states in particular barred the road of Russian expansion. To the south ruled the khan of the Crimea, controlling access to the Black Sea. His raiders cast greedy glances at the wealth of Moscow, and he arrogantly demanded to be bought off with Muscovite gold. From the Volga to the Ural Mountains stretched the khanate of Kazan, and beyond the Urals, on Asian soil, still other Tatar chieftains held forth in their yurt capitals.

As is always the way of conquerors, the sons of Genghis Khan's warriors had intermarried with conquered tribes—with Cumans, Ukrainians and Great Russians. Along the way, many cultural traits had been adopted from them. Of greatest significance was their conversion to the faith of the Prophet Muhammad, thereby joining them to a religious community stretching from China to North Africa.

The world of Islam was dominated by the Turkish Empire, which was then at the peak of its power and claimed nominal overlordship over all the Tatar states. It was ruled by Sultan Suleiman the Magnificent, perhaps the most brilliant monarch of the century. He controlled more land than the Byzantine emperors had, and Constantinople, his capital, adorned with the peaked spires of countless mosques, had few rivals in splendor and wealth. The Tatars looked to the Muslim Sultan for assistance. They well knew his ambition to spread Turkish rule farther northward into the Russian forests.

All this Ivan had to take into consideration as he pondered Russia's course of action. Fearing that the blustering demands of the Crimean khan might be followed up by the threatened invasion, he dispatched an army to meet his. The khan had indeed marched northward toward Moscow, but when his scouts reported the approach of a Russian force, the Tatars retreated in haste, leaving behind a camp full of food and costly ornaments. In his flight the khan even abandoned his harem and his camels. Treasure, women and animals were quickly dispatched to Moscow. The Muscovites gave only cursory glances to the other booty. Their main fascination was riveted on the hump-backed camels, never before seen in the capital. The Czar was presented with the khan's own camel, a specimen of rare beauty. But when it refused to kneel at his command, he had it killed. Perhaps this taught the other camels a lesson.

It had been proved once more that Tatars liked sudden attacks by overwhelming numbers, but had little stomach for prolonged campaigns where the chances were more even. They melted into the semiarid steppes that stretch between the Caspian and the Black Sea, and the Russians did not pursue them there for fear of bringing the Turkish giant into the fray. Ivan could chalk this up as a victory of sorts, but it was more a temporary stand-off, nothing that would raise him to the stature of a national hero in the eyes of his people.

Though not a warrior by nature, he fully realized that he would have to add sizable territories to his inherited possessions. Only in this way could he make nobles and commoners alike bow to his command.

A target for an impressive military conquest had to be found.

All signs pointed to Tatar-held Kazan. Only 150 miles southeast of Moscow, this Volga city had long been a wealthy commercial center, a crossroads of trade along the river from the northern forests to the warm Crimea and, by road and river portages, from the west to the Urals and beyond.

Sometimes in accord with other Tatar states, sometimes at odds with them, the Kazan Tatars made it a regular habit to raid Russian towns and villages. At the moment, some five thousand Russians were held prisoner in the city, waiting to be sold at Turkish and Persian slave markets.

Russians expected their Czar to lead them against Kazan. They felt insecure behind a frontier protected only by wooden stockades strung out, at best, a day's ride apart. They wanted to rescue their enslaved sons and daughters. Even more important, war against the infidel Tatars would be a religious crusade: the cross against the crescent, Christ against Muhammad. Already the Turks had carried the green standards of the Prophet to the gates of Vienna. The Muslim wave threatened to engulf beleaguered Christianity from the south and from the east.

"Carry the cross against the heathens, O Czar," admonished Sylvester in his best Old Testament posture. "Destroy the abominations which they call their temples of worship. Complete the task of repentance for your sins and for the sins of your people."

Ivan knew he had to follow the call, yet he hesitated. Always fearful for his own safety, he had never shown any talent for military strategy. He was no Alexander, no Julius Caesar, although he lavishly admired those ancient heroes.

And more important, Ivan had no army. Up to that time, war had been waged in the feudal manner, now outmoded everywhere west of Russia. The grand prince called on his fellow-princes and boyars to come with their vassals and serving men and do his fighting. They came if and when they felt like it. There was no long-range strategy, no military discipline.

Commands were distributed among the heads of the ranking families. To show courage was virtuous, to obey orders demeaning.

The Russians rode to war on unshod horses, with curved swords and axes hanging from their saddles. Bridle and bow were held in the left hand, sword and whip in the right. When the rider shot, he dropped sword and whip, which were fastened to a strap.

From their enemies, the Tatars, the Russians had learned the tactic of massed attack preceded by clouds of arrows. They moved in with axes swinging, yelling at the tops of their voices while trumpets and drums raised the noise level incredibly.

Sustained maneuvering was not part of the fighting manual. If the attack failed to rout the enemy, the survivors retreated to wait for another day. But the Russian fighting man had one superb quality—his incredible endurance under grinding hardships. He traveled long distances carrying a bag of millet, pork and salt which sustained him for many days, and he could sleep on the ground with no cover but his long cloak.

Ivan's reform work progressed at increased speed. With every passing day it became more evident that a complete overhaul of the military must be given top priority. A standing armed force was needed, answerable only to the Czar, not only to fight the Tatars but also to enforce his will over recalcitrant subjects at home.

The serving nobility was tapped to furnish the officers corps. A permanent force of infantry was created, the *streltsi*, made up of commoners and of foreign mercenaries. They were equipped with the recently invented arquebuses. These handguns had to be loaded through the muzzle with powder and a large bullet, and fired with the help of a matchlock. An experienced archer could aim better and shoot farther; but the noisy, flashing guns had a demoralizing effect on the enemy who did not possess them.

The cavalry was strengthened by hired bands of mounted Cossacks, and as for artillery, Ivan saw to it that his forces possessed one of the best of the time. He hired German and Dutch cannon-makers, who trained the Russians in the art of maintaining and using the new weaponry.

A formidable fighting force was emerging, eager to test its skill and courage. Still the Czar lingered on in his capital. Small units were sent out to engage the enemy, and several indecisive engagements were fought. Sarcastic verses began to be passed from mouth to mouth chiding Ivan for his hesitance.

The whole relationship between Moscow and Kazan was confused. When the Tatar stronghold was beset by inner dissension, Moscow had, for a time, forced it into nominal submission. Tatar factions had gone over to the Russian side and fought against their own kin. But now Kazan was unified again and determined to resist. Its hopes rested on rumors of Russia's inner weaknesses and on expected help from the Crimea and from the Turkish Sultan. A formal demand of surrender was sent to Khan Ediger of Kazan. Contemptuously he answered the Czar, "All is ready for you here. We invite you to the feast."

After this affront to his dignity, which soon became public knowledge, Ivan could no longer procrastinate. Preparations went into high gear. Huge stores were shipped down the Volga to a supply base just opposite Kazan. Lumber arrived with which to build living quarters, warehouses and churches. The base grew into a complete new city named Svyazhsk.

The day of departure came. After having borne two daughters, the Czarina was again pregnant. She followed her husband into the cathedral and, as the divine liturgy was chanted, prayed loud for victory and for his safe return.

Gingerly the Czar lifted her from her knees. "My beloved, look after my people while I am gone. Take from the treasury and give to the poor and the sick." He handed her a bundle of long iron keys. "Here are the keys to the prisons. Free anybody

whom you would like to see free, no matter what their crime.
Keep well, and pray for the birth of a son."

He mounted his richly bedecked horse. The venerable Macary
accompanied him to the city gate, followed by chanting priests
and monks. Then he rode on at the head of the *streltsi*, the
Cossacks and the nobles. Princes and boyars forgot their quarrels
for the moment. Nobody wanted to miss the holy crusade.

At every town the inhabitants waited in the streets to bless
the fighters. Everywhere local lords and their armed retainers
fell in with the steadily growing host.

Quickly the environs of Kazan were cleared of roving Tatars.
Vastly outnumbered by the approaching enemy, the khan's hundred thousand warriors were asked once more to surrender. Shouting curses and blasphemies at the Christian God, they refused.
There was no attempt to defend the city proper. As the Russians
entered the outlying streets, the inhabitants fled into the spacious
inner fortress, the Kazan Kremlin, and crowded into the Khan's
palace and the mosques, stables and soldiers' barracks. Earthworks
and towers protected the stronghold. It held ample provisions,
and several wells supplied all the needed water.

The siege was on, but the early spirit of elation among the
attackers was put to severe tests. The nobles took up their old
quarrels, and the soldiers spent the idle days drinking and
carousing. Scurvy decimated the ranks, and to top off all the
trials, a catastrophic gale, accompanied by torrential rains, turned
the camp into a sea of mud. Tents were blown away, supplies
scattered, food ruined.

The men who had marched out in high spirits had become
a bedraggled, grimy ragtag assemblage. Had the beleaguered
Tatars recognized their advantage and sallied out in force, the
campaign would have come to an end right then. But they stuck
to their ramparts, except for small-scale sallies in which their
curved sabers, light lances and speedy arrows thinned the Russian ranks even further.

For Ivan it was a foregone conclusion that all the misfortune was the result of sorcery and of evil spells cast by the enemy. He was determined to counter with weapons of the same kind. He ordered fresh provisions rushed to the camp from all over Russia. In addition, the barges and wagons brought priests carrying a huge cross famed widely for its power to work miracles.

"They brought the holy cross," wrote Andrei Kurbsky, one of the commanders and a close friend of Ivan, "into which had been inserted a piece of the Savior's wood, and thanks to the power of the life-giving cross, straightaway from that hour onward all trace of the pagan magic disappeared."

The crusading zeal was rekindled in the troops. With haste they repaired the camp. The pace of the siege quickened.

The inner fortress of Kazan was now so completely encircled that not a soul could pass in or out. Sappers tunneled by night underneath the ramparts and left there large charges of gunpowder prepared by Dutch engineers. The explosions tore breeches in the walls, but the defenders filled them with their own bodies.

Trapped in their stronghold, the Tatars tried to cool their frustrations by desperate sorties. Few ever returned. Some who had been taken prisoner by the Russians were tied to stakes facing the besieged and made to exort their compatriots, "Surrender, brothers. Your resistance is hopeless. Beseech the Czar for mercy. He grants you free exit."

By now the defenders of Kazan had likewise worked themselves into a frenzy of religious fanaticism. They aimed their arrows at their own countrymen, the helpless prisoners, shouting, "Better to die by a clean Muslim arrow than by the hands of the tainted Christians."

All through the night of October 2, 1552, the sappers dug into the hill under the Kremlin of Kazan. More barrels of powder than ever before were dragged through the winding shaft. The explosion was to be the signal for the final assault.

Long before dawn the Czar was awake in his pavilion of gold cloth. He knelt before the icon of St. Sergius surrounded by priests and by his commanders.

A tremendous thunder shook the ground as if the innards of the earth itself had erupted. Debris was flying as far as the edge of the camp. The moment was here.

Nervously the officers waited for the Czar to get up off the floor, where he lay prostrated. "Come, Your Majesty," urged Prince Michael Vorotinsky, the chief commander. "We must use the advantage. Every minute is valuable."

Ivan remained immobile except in his lips, which continued to murmur prayers. The commander sighed, turned away and drew his sword. The attack was on.

The magic cross moved forward carried on many sturdy shoulders. Lighted lanterns and candles in the hands of long-bearded priests cast ghostly shadows in the predawn grayness.

Behind the black standard with the double-headed eagle, the nobles and their armed men surged up the slope. Their yells mingled with the sound of trumpets and drums into an infernal crescendo of noise. Behind them, teams of foot soldiers carried huge wooden shields with holes through which muskets were fired.

The siege towers, some forty feet high, began to rumble towards the enemy. From their highest platforms, burning arrows whistled through the air, setting fires in many places. The defenders fought back with boiling oil and with big boulders sent hurtling down on the invaders.

The first Russian units storming through the breeches forgot all caution. They were made up of untrained liegemen in the service of the nobility. Contrary to instructions, they dispersed into the buildings, and soon they were weighted down with pillaged gold, silver and precious cloth. In their greed they did not notice that the enemy had managed to regroup. The men of Kazan took a frightening toll of the looters. With victory almost in its grasp, the Russian army faced chaos and defeat.

But the planners of the final battle had taken precautions. The *streltsi*, well trained and disciplined, had been held in reserve. Now they advanced in good order. Their attack carried them over piles of corpses into the innermost court. The battle was won; the fifty-day siege was over.

Only when servants pointed out to the still prostrate Czar the flames rising from the Khan's own palace did he finally rise from the ground. Surrounded by his large personal bodyguard, he rode into captured Kazan.

The killing of the vanquished was still in progress. In one of his rare shows of pity, Ivan called for a halt. "They are not Christians," he said, "but they are men."

The captive khan was brought before him in chains. "You may keep your life and your freedom, Ediger," said the Czar as he raised the vanquished foe from his knees. "You have fought bravely. But you must accept the Christian faith. You have seen today the strength of our God and of His saints."

Not having a choice, the Khan accepted the condition.

Immediately orders were given to destroy all mosques and to consecrate a piece of ground for a future cathedral. It was cleared of corpses and rubble, and on the same evening, after a stately procession around the broken walls, a *Te Deum* was held there, a service of thanks to God, who had granted victory.

Now twenty-two years old, the monarch indeed felt he was heaven's favorite. Hardly had the noise of battle subsided when a messenger rode up at top speed with the news that the Czarina had given birth to a son. The heir to the throne, so long and impatiently awaited, had arrived. Impulsively Ivan jumped from his horse and kissed the startled bringer of good tidings. He took off his own bejeweled cloak and draped it as a present over the servant's shoulders.

Much work still remained to be done in the ruined city. To become a Russian stronghold, it had to be rebuilt and settled with Russian officials, merchants and a strong garrison. Tatar bands still roamed the neighborhood, and nobody knew what the Crimean Khan would do now and even less what the Sultan in Constantinople had in mind.

The victors had enough wisdom to pardon the survivors of Kazan, even to encourage those who had fled into the forest to return. They were promised safety provided they pledged loyalty to the new ruler.

But all these problems held no interest for Ivan. He was anxious to be off, though his commanders strongly urged him to stay on. Within a week he was on his way up the Volga towards Moscow.

The trip turned into a triumphal march, so glorious, so rich in popular outpouring of pride and enthusiasm that he bridled his impatience to thoroughly savor the joy of it. In every settlement along the way, the population knelt in his path with candles and holy images, celebrating him as if he had descended straight from heaven.

Kazan's fall was the victory of the cross over the crescent. The Muslim advance had come to a halt. The day of vengeance had arrived for the long sufferings under the yoke of the Golden Horde. Europe's mightiest stream, the Volga, had become a Russian highway. The young nation was reaching out with hopes of limitless grandeur.

Anastasia, accompanied by the Metropolitan and all the clergy, met her returning hero husband at Sretenka Gate. He dismounted, and together they entered the city square, which was ablaze with bunting and flowers. All the church bells were ringing. The royal couple could barely make its way through the mass of cheering people into the palace. Chamberlains led them to their private quarters, where stood the crib of the Czarevich Dmitri.

On the streets the minstrels sang new songs about Ivan Vasile-vich, the victor of Kazan, although he had personally contributed little to the victory, except for boosting the morale of the fighters by his presence. The chroniclers compared him to Charlemagne, who, centuries earlier and also not quite deservedly, had been given credit for stopping the Muslim advance into Western Europe.

The Czar himself eagerly endorsed the heroic role attributed to him by all this acclaim. He felt the need to commemorate this accomplishment with a unique monument. What could be more appropriate than to build still another cathedral and dedicate it to Russia's favorite spokesmen in heaven, St. Basil the Blessed?

And so a structure began to take shape that the world had never seen before—not inside the Kremlin, where already stood three cathedrals, but on the south end of Red Square, silhouetted against the Moskva River.

Ever since, visitors have been gaping at the sight with a mix-ture of admiration and bewilderment. It is a cluster of nine chapels, octagonal in shape, mounted on a high platform, each different in style and height, each crowned by a different-shaped and-colored dome. In splendid isolation, St. Basil's Cathedral stands at the edge of the giant square, dark brick-red below and a soaring symphony of gold, blue and green above.

To reach the effect of spectacular diversity, the architect Barma Postnik blended Persian, Indian and Byzantine styles. Yet the total impact remained distinctly Russian. A legend persists that the Czar had the eyes of the builder put out so that he would never be able to duplicate his famed creation, but this is one atrocity of which Ivan the Terrible stands innocent.

7
THE "ENGLISH CZAR"

The victory flowers were wilted, the bunting soggy from the persistent spring rains. In the shops and stalls, voices were subdued and worried.

"Any news about the Czar?" was the inevitable question when a newcomer entered. "Is it really serious? Is he dying?"

Some claimed to have heard that his body was covered with boils, that he had contracted the plague, that he was already dead but that the court kept it a secret.

Jubilation had abruptly turned into sorrow.

In the royal bedroom, near the enormous porcelain heating stove, stood the massive bedstead piled high with down blankets. Under the canopy lay the Czar, face wet with perspiration, eyes burning with fever. Cramps shook his body in short, violent spasms.

Nobody knew what had brought on the sudden illness. It could not have been lack of cleanliness. Like most Russians, Ivan spent long hours in the bathhouse. He sat in the sweat chamber and in the hot tubs, and he struck his body with switches and twigs to produce more perspiration. Then, as was the general custom, he would jump into ice-cold water or even roll naked in the snow, depending on the season.

This radical purification process could have induced pneumonia even in a stronger body than the Czar's, or his digestive system could have collapsed under the strain of the frequent fasts followed by bouts of overeating and overdrinking.

Whatever it was, the usual stories of evil spells quickly made the rounds while Sylvester, true to form, described the sickness as God's punishment. Inclined to the latter diagnosis, Ivan swore to undertake an especially long and arduous pilgrimage should recovery be granted him.

But for the time, the prospects looked dim. Candles were kept burning around the bed while monks chanted endless litanies. No opportunity was to be missed, so magicians and sorcerers were also called in to perform their rites. Among all this din and agitation, the patient grew weaker by the hour.

The Metropolitan came to administer the last rites of the church. As he bent over the wasted young body, he urged the ruler to bring his earthly affairs in order. A will had to be made without delay.

In a voice which was hardly audible, Ivan called for his aides and for the top-ranking boyars. His head was propped up by stout pillows. Feebly he tried to raise his hand, which clutched a golden cross.

"I am dying, gentlemen, but Russia must go on. Kiss the cross and swear loyalty to my son, Dmitri, the next czar."

The answer was stark silence. The smoke of candles and the smell of sickness lay heavily upon the boyars. They looked at the haggard body of their sovereign and then looked at each other.

Again the wheezing voice from the sickbed urged: "Kiss the cross for my son as you have kissed it for me."

The silence broke. Loud, angry controversy erupted among the lords of the realm. Impatiently Prince Zakharin, Anastasia's uncle, shouted, "Haven't you heard? Do the Czar's will. Pledge loyalty to Dmitri."

"But he is only an infant," countered another prince. "Have you forgotten the bloodshed, the ruinous strife when Ivan succeeded his father to the throne?"

Nobody, including the Czar himself, thought of his brother, Yuri, whose mental defectiveness was known to all.

It was clear that the boyars had talked this matter over long before being called into the Czar's presence, and all the evidence pointed at a deep and dangerous division among them.

The spokesman of one faction proposed, "We want Vladimir, the Czar's cousin. He will command respect. At least he is a grown man." Vladimir Andreyewich, a prince of high lineage, had distinguished himself before Kazan as a commander. Had Ivan no son, he would have been the undisputed successor. As soon as he heard of the illness, he had begun bribing and propositioning many boyars. Several had promised him their support. Ivan knew of his cousin's ambitions. Panic shook his feverish body. He was well aware how pretenders to the throne were apt to deal with relatives who stood in the way. "Promise me," he implored his nobles like a lowly petitioner. "Promise me to protect the lives of my wife and son. Swear that you will not let them come to harm."

They did not listen. He was forgotten, as if already dead.

Macary urged them to leave the sickroom. Without interrupting their loud dispute, they filed into an anteroom.

Ivan lay exhausted. All the fears and agonies of his childhood surged back into his delirious mind. He could trust nobody. A pack of hungry wolves surrounded him, waiting only for the victim to breathe his last breath.

Where were his aides whom he had raised from obscurity to power? They had remained silent. Adashev's father had spoken out against the infant's succession, and the son had not rebuked him. As for Sylvester, he had openly questioned the wisdom of the Czar's demand. Nobody had supported him, except his wife's unpopular relatives, and they only because they hoped to reap wealth and high positions should Anastasia become regent.

Summoning his last resources of strength, he sat up. Servants propped more cushions against his sagging back. He was not dead yet. He was still the emperor, heir to Caesar and the exalted monarchs of Constantinople. "Call them back," he cried feebly.

They filed back, confused and fearful. What if Ivan was not to die after all? Who would be safe then from his vengeance? Macary assumed the role of peacemaker. "Remember the honors you have received from Czar Ivan. Remember how God has favored you with victory and wealth under his rule."

One boyar stepped forward to kiss the cross. Another followed. Then they all came. Nobody wanted to stay behind, but the expressions on their faces mirrored reluctance. They performed the act as an empty gesture, to be quickly forgotten after the ruler had been laid to rest in the cathedral of the Archangel Michael.

For weeks the sickness burned in the ravaged body. For weeks the people prayed in countless churches for their Little Father. He was, at that time, truly beloved by the masses of his subjects.

Then the fever subsided. The Czar rose from his sickbed. As all human events were thought to be part of God's plan, his recovery was hailed as a miracle, and nobody believed more fervently than Ivan himself in God's direct intercession. Still weak, walking with shaky legs, he set the date of departure on the pilgrimage which he had promised. The trip was to take him to the monastery of St. Kiril, which lay on the frozen coast of the White Sea.

All advisers counseled against the trip. The monk Maxim the Greek, with whom he liked to engage in religious disputes, lectured him: "The fulfillment of unwise promises is not acceptable to God."

Ivan was not convinced.

"God is everywhere," the monk reasoned, "in Moscow as well as at St. Kiril. Give thanks by staying and preparing another crusade against the infidel Muslims." Even Maxim's prediction that little Dmitri would die if Ivan went through with the voyage did not deter the Czar from his goal.

The journey through the damp chill of spring was grueling despite the joyful greeting the recovered sovereign received everywhere. Many shrines were visited. Long hours were spent in conversations with learned monks whose intelligence could furnish a welcome challenge for Ivan.

The hermit Vassayan told him: "By nature the Czar is like all other men, but in authority he is like the highest God." Such statements gladdened Ivan's heart. He wanted more of the same.

"How do I go about translating this lofty idea into the practice of daily government?" he inquired.

"Never have anybody about you except people who are less intelligent than yourself. Keep the rule that thou art the person to teach, but not to be taught. Order and be obeyed."

"I will remember these words. I will heed them from now on."

But what he should have heeded at the time was Maxim the Greek's warning. Dragged through the rain and the howling winds, rocked to sleep in cold, drafty halls, little Dmitri fell sick. This time there was no miracle. His tiny corpse was carried back to Moscow for burial. In retrospect, how ridiculous seemed all the wrangling over Dmitri's succession.

A sobered and embittered Ivan reentered the Kremlin. He looked much older than his twenty-three years, and the Czarina was ill with exhaustion and grief.

The Czar threw himself into an intensive program of activity as if to drown his personal disappointments. Outwardly there was no change in his attitude towards Sylvester, Adashev and others who had not measured up to his expectations at the crucial moment. They continued in their privileged roles. Sylvester became more and more uncompromising. He practically identified himself with the Almighty and threatened everybody, including the emperor, with hellfire and damnation whenever his advice was not completely accepted. Ivan listened, but became less and less inclined to obey.

In the following years the work of reform was resumed. The

goal, a centralized, authoritarian and multinational state, still lay in the future, but progress was being made at a respectable rate. Already Moscow's rule extended far beyond the limits of the Great Russian nationality. It embraced Tatars, Baskirs, Nogais and others.

The streamlining of the cumbersome governmental machinery continued. Once overlapping functions were assigned to new departments, each headed by a *dyak,* or secretary, who was frequently selected from the lower nobility or even from the ranks of the commoners. The outlines of a cabinet began to emerge.

At a time when Erasmus, Rabelais and Montaigne were stirring western Europe with their writings, Ivan felt deeply about the backwardness of his nation. No pen inside Russia was creating anything even vaguely comparable. Not a single printing press existed until Ivan personally commissioned a German printer to build one in 1553. The first work off the press was a pious biography of St. Basil entitled *The Apostle.*

Russia was equally deficient in technical and commercial progress despite the native shrewdness and perseverance of its traders. Ivan encouraged western craftsmen to settle in his cities, and he welcomed western merchants provided he could keep their activities under strict supervision.

In the last analysis, everything in the country belonged to the ruler. This was the ultimate in the concept of the authoritarian state. The practical consequence was strict government regulation of trade and a long list of crown monopolies, of which the most lucrative was the making and dispensing of alcoholic beverages.

On the one hand the church thundered against the evils of drunkenness, but on the other the government encouraged it, provided the tippling was done in licensed taverns. Only when the customers overindulged were they picked up at night from the gutter. In the morning the local judge then fined them two rubles and had them whipped in the marketplace.

From the Tatars, Russian princes had learned the usefulness of maintaining an efficient network of spies and informers. Reports came in from a most unlikely place which aroused the Czar's immediate interest. They originated in St. Nicholas Monastery, a forlorn outpost in the northernmost reaches of the empire where the ground is eternally frozen under a thin layer of earth. It was not a place which usually generated a lot of exciting news.

With astonishment Ivan read the message:

A large ship built like no other that has ever been seen came sailing from the open ocean into the protection of St. Nicholas Bay and cast anchor by the mouth of the Dvina River. Nobody knows where the crew came from. Nobody can understand them, nor can they understand us. We have given them fresh water and food, because they were sick and emaciated. What shall be done with them, *Hospodi* [Lord]?

The Czar thought long. He was inclined to distrust anybody, especially strangers. But he was also intensely curious. To converse with foreigners held a lifelong fascination. "From where could they come?" he pondered. He ruled out the lands of Tatars, Turks, Poles or Scandinavians. His people would have been familiar with all those nationalities.

At last he gave orders, "Take horses, sleighs, warm clothing and ample stocks of food. Make haste and conduct the strangers to me. Treat them well, but see that they are kept from any contact with the peasants and townsmen along the way."

When the detachment of soldiers arrived at the mouth of the Dvina, they found the mysterious travelers in good health. The local people had at first fled from them, fearing they were ghosts risen from the sea. Later there was friendly banter back and forth, but no exchange of goods, even though the sailors had wanted to barter. No trading without the Czar's permission: this rule had been beaten into even these remote subjects, and they knew the penalties.

The visitors themselves had no idea where their course had taken them, nor were they aware that the trek to Moscow was to be 1,500 miles. They had lost count of time and distance.

In the military escort was a Scandinavian, a man who had roamed about a great deal and who knew many languages. He tried them all out on the men who were half guests and half captives, until he hit upon the right one—English.

During the long days of slow progress on barges and on portage roads, the interpreter talked with the leader of the band, who called himself Captain Chancellor. For the first time the captain found out that he was in Russia and that his destination was Moscow, seat of Ivan Vasilevich.

The Englishman may have been surprised about the information he received, but it was he who had the most remarkable tale to tell. This was a time when his country was still a second-rate seapower, outdistanced by Spain in colonies and in fighting ships. Spanish galleons controlled access to the New World and to the fabled wealth of Cathay, which, ever since Marco Polo's voyage, all western explorers had hoped to reach.

Seeing their ambitions blocked, the British, a nation of merchants and sailors, sought for an alternative route. As they studied their grossly inaccurate maps, they wondered, "Why not bypass the odious Spaniards? Why not sail eastward over the roof of the European continent?"

Three ships set out to find the fabled northeast passage. Two foundered in icy storms, and their crews froze to death. Only the *Bonaventura,* skippered by Captain Chancellor, managed to limp into St. Nicholas Bay. The crew was bruised with frostbite and sick from exhaustion, but it never wavered in its determination to pursue the route to Cathay.

Swift couriers related the story to the Czar. He had heard of

England, but had only a vague idea where it was and who ruled it. He knew that the British embraced some sort of Christianity and that they were not his enemies. There was no reason to worry.

Muscovites turned out in large numbers to stare at the new arrivals. They had never seen so many men with clean-shaven faces and with such unfamiliar clothing: short jackets which left the legs, encased in tight-fitting breeches, exposed to sight. It seemed indecent. The armed escort saw to it that nobody came too close to the visitors.

For many days, the Englishmen were not allowed outside their quarters. Friendly bearded men brought them ample supplies. "The Czar sends you meat and wine from his own table," they said. "Eat and drink all you can."

Chancellor suspected that their hosts, who seemed to double as their jailers, tried to get them drunk in order to learn all their secrets. His repeated requests to see their master were brushed off with such excuses as "The Czar is with his troops" or "The Czar is ill—have patience."

Finally an audience was granted. Servants brought costly garments from the Kremlin so that the guests could appear appropriately attired in long coats trimmed with fur and gold and in finely tooled leather boots. They were helped into the saddles of richly bedecked horses.

Before the convoy departed they were given detailed instructions about proper court behavior: Prostrate yourself before the Czar. Never remove your eyes from his person. Don't address him unless he first speaks to you.

On Red Square there was a long, unexplained delay. Only later Chancellor found out that Ivan had ordered it so he could secretly watch them from a window before meeting them face to face.

The audience was staged with unusual pomp to impress the guests. From his throne, the emperor, surrounded by his family and in the presence of the boyars and *dyaks,* graciously inquired about the health of his beloved brother, King Edward VI. He was unaware that "his beloved brother" had died in the meantime and had been succeeded by Queen Mary I.

The audience was short, but Ivan bade his guests stay for the banquet. They were led to the bathhouse, where they received the full treatment of the sweatchamber, the beating with birch switches and the dunking in the ice-cold tub. Then they were given fresh garments. When they entered the banquet hall, they saw two hundred courtiers seated according to family and rank. The Czar too wore new garments, and his gold crown had been replaced by a silver one.

"Come and eat bread," said the sovereign. It was the traditional formula of hospitality. He crossed himself, broke bread and dipped it in salt. To the surprise of the visitors, he called everybody by name, whereupon servants distributed the pieces.

Then the feasting began in earnest. A small army of attendants marched in, each carrying a huge tray. A chamberlain preceded them with a swan on a golden platter. He placed it before the emperor, carved it and then tasted a tiny piece to make sure that it was not poisoned. The Czar's plate was filled and then those of the guests.

Course followed course, all served with equal ceremony and all pretasted for security's sake. There were baked meat and fish, soup seasoned with onions and garlic, many varieties of beets and cabbage and all sorts of fruit and sweets.

The banquet extended from noon into the late afternoon. When the sun set, candles were brought in in golden candelabra. The company toasted the two monarchs and each other with strong spirits. In mounting astonishment the Englishmen observed the bearded Russians kissing each other heartily each time they emptied their goblets. Chancellor's men found banqueting with the Russians almost as strenuous as searching for the northeast passage.

More audiences followed, longer and less formal, in which the Czar tried to familiarize himself with many aspects of English life. He was especially eager to learn about commercial ventures, about banking and credit practices and about the highly profitable trade in oriental wares. At long last, Chancellor was dismissed with abundant presents and with letters of friendship to the British sovereign. Embellished with flowery expressions of brotherly love, the letters clearly expressed the wish for permanent trade relations and for the exchange of ambassadors.

In 1555 Chancellor was back in Moscow, bringing big news. Mary, the new queen, had recently married Philip, King of Spain and ruler of the New World, thereby creating the most formidable power complex in existence, extending to both sides of the Atlantic Ocean. This unnatural combination was not to last for long, but nobody knew that at the time.

Ivan was only mildly interested in those dynastic affairs. Much more important for him was that with Chancellor had arrived a Mr. George Killingworth, the first agent of the newly chartered Russia Company. British capitalists had grasped the enormous possibilities of trade in Russian flax and hemp and, above all, in Russian fur. Even more tempting was the prospect of transit trade with the lands beyond Ivan's realm from whence came silk, tea and spices, all fetching staggering profits on the European markets.

The Queen was persuaded to grant a charter to the new trading company with privileges similar to those held by the Hudson's Bay Company and the British East India Company. These privileges gave the companies power to act almost like independent states.

Far from begrudging the franchises of the new Russia Company, Ivan showered it with a number of additional privileges. A long document stated in part:

We, for us, our heirs and successors, do by these presents give and grant free license, faculty, authority and power unto the said governor, assistants and community for the said fellowship and their successors for ever, that all and singular the merchants of the same company may at all times hereafter, freely and safely with their ships and goods sail, come and enter into all and singular our lands, and there buy, sell, barter and change all kind of merchandize with all manner of merchants and people freely and quietly without any restraint. . . .

The generous terms granted the Russia Company contrasted sharply with the restrictions under which the Czar's own subjects had to operate. He foresaw the advantages that would result for the royal treasury and for the national economy in general. To make him more amenable, Killingworth presented the Czar with several handsomely crafted firearms for his vast gun collection, but the main cargo of the expedition consisted of samples of the famous English broadcloth. With this as inducement for barter, the company prepared to push eastward toward the ancient caravan stops of Samarkand and Bukhara, where the bazaars exhibited the treasures of Persia, India and China.

It took many long sessions to hammer out the details of the new commercial relationship. Ivan was obviously impressed by the worldly-wise, logical, hard-bargaining Englishmen, but he was a shrewd bargainer himself, and he granted them privileges not only out of personal sympathy. After an especially hard negotiating session, the British agent sighed in despair, "No Russian believes anything that is said to him or says anything that is worthy of belief." In the end, the new relationship secured for Russia such greatly needed items as iron, lead, gunpowder and other war materials, together with the technicians who could put them to use.

All foreign trade remained an exclusive state monopoly and a very lucrative one to boot. Recognizing the fantastic possibilities of this trade, the British were willing to pay exorbitant prices, such as three hundred pounds sterling for a fine black fox skin. They had stumbled upon the richest reservoir of sable, ermine and blue fox in the world. The Russian trade became lucrative

beyond all expectations and repaid manyfold any presents the
visitors had brought along and any prices they paid for the furs.
But the Czar's treasury also grew heavy from the returns of such
transactions, and it was a very welcome source of much-needed
revenue.

Once the business part of their association was concluded, Ivan
enjoyed the company of the Englishmen in a warm personal way.
Dr. Standish, who had accompanied the British delegation, became his court physician and, besides receiving a salary, was
showered with such gifts as a sable coat, a sleigh with bearskin
seats and a magnificent pair of horses.

Other foreigners came and found a friendly welcome from the
Kremlin: German army deserters, Dutch Protestants fleeing
religious persecution, rebels and adventurers of all sorts. A suburb
of Moscow was set aside for them, and their know-how was used
to advance Russian skills. But the English remained the Czar's
favorites.

Chancellor stayed on for months and was often called to court
for long, intimate chats. A close friendship also developed between the Czar and Anthony Jenkinson, who succeeded Killingworth as the agent of the Russia Company. Pursuing the
company's goal of a land route to Cathay, Jenkinson traveled to
Central Asia. On his return to Moscow, he brought Ivan, among
many odd gifts, the tail of a yak, the beast of burden in the
Tibetan highlands.

In time, Jenkinson managed to completely eliminate the
competition of other foreigners in trade. Englishmen crossed the
Muscovite empire in all directions, using the horses of the official
pony express. They prospected for Russian minerals and even
minted English money in Russian mints.

Like Chancellor before him, Jenkinson was a frequent guest
at the Kremlin, where Ivan plied him with endless questions.
Discussions between Czar and Britisher had to be carried out
through interpreters, since Ivan did not learn any foreign lan-

guages. Patiently he listened to the tales of British inventiveness and daring, but he shook his head in dismay when told about the British political system. Such things as Magna Carta and Parliament were beyond his range of understanding. "What a way to run a country," he thought. "It could never work here. I know my Russians."

Nor could he understand why Britishers preferred to be ruled by women. In Russia men used the whip on them; in England they put them on the throne. He was informed that Queen Mary had died and had been succeeded by another female ruler, a young girl named Elizabeth. He did not hide his strong disapproval. But since there was nothing he could do about it and since he wanted to continue the happy relationship with England, he sent Elizabeth his best wishes and instructed his ambassador to give her some costly gems as presents. The Queen was pleased and reciprocated with a complicated mechanical clock and a pair of lion cubs. It became a favorite pastime of strolling Muscovites to stare at the beasts as they growlingly wandered back and forth in the Kremlin moat.

At the court in Moscow, sarcastic remarks made the rounds about the ruler who preferred the company of foreigners to that of his own countrymen. Behind his back they mockingly called him the "English Czar."

Both Chancellor and Jenkinson wrote accounts of their travels which have become important sources for the study of conditions under Ivan IV. In their reports we read not only of Russian crudeness and backwardness, but also of the enormous potential power in that giant who was still half asleep. Prophetically, Chancellor wrote:

If they knew their strength, no man were able to make match with them, nor they that dwell near them should have rest of them.

8
IVAN GROZNI

The Czar bent over a number of maps which were spread on the low table, gifts of his English friends. The large scrolls had been unrolled and tacked to the wood. They showed the continents in grossly misshapen outlines. The distances across the oceans were too short. All sorts of nonexistent islands and fantastic sea creatures had been drawn into the blue spaces representing the world-girdling seas.

Ivan's interest, at the moment, was focused not on the endless ocean but on the outlines of the European countries, and these were fairly accurate. Reared in mental isolation, he was just now becoming aware that there, between the western boundaries of his own country and the shores of the Atlantic, lay the real playground of monarchs. The map before him represented the chessboard of the political power game.

An obsession gripped the Russian monarch. He must enter that game, and to do that he would first have to master its rules. With the intensity which characterized his whole being, he studied the maps and tried to understand the meanings of all the lines and dots and fanciful symbols. The picture of the European political scene, in all its complications and contradictions, began to take shape before his inner eye.

The most advanced European nations were battling each other
not only on the crowded soil of the continent, but even more
viously on the wide oceans. Spain and Portugal ruled vast
overseas empires, and England was fast becoming their determined rival, full of confidence in the quickly growing power
of her fleet. But this was only one facet of the vastly complex
political panorama. While British "sea dogs" chased Spanish
treasure ships in the Caribbean, the island kingdom was also
locked in an age-old struggle with France, her neighbor across
the Channel. Both countries had recently begun to emerge from
the feudal disunity of the Middle Ages. They were on the way to
becoming strongly centralized states, and were flexing their
national muscles, seeking glory and expansion beyond their borders.

For these two and for other countries, there were always plenty
of excuses to interfere with the chaotic conditions of Central
Europe, which was nominally united in an oversized common-
wealth called the Holy Roman Empire. Actually it was, as one
historian remarked, neither Roman nor holy nor an empire, but
a patchwork of principalities and city states which were constantly feuding with each other. The emperor of the paper empire
was receiving all sorts of ceremonial honors. It cost nothing to
bestow them, but beyond the territories which he controlled
directly by the mercenary troops in his personal pay, he exercised
no power.

Fierce rivalries were rending the Holy Roman Empire asunder
from one end to the other. The wealthy northern Italian city
states, Venice, Florence and the rest, were at one another's throats
with deadly weapons and with all the tricks of commercial rivalry.
Often their enmity was directed against the Pope, who not only
was the spiritual head of western Christianity, but also ruled
over large territories in central Italy. French and Spanish rulers
fished in those troubled waters. They sent armies across the Alps,
and these soldiers of fortune, after attending mass and receiving

communion according to the Catholic rite, saw nothing wrong with raping and plundering Rome, the holy city, itself.

While Italy was ravaged by contending armies in the pay of kings, popes and merchant republics, conflict and economic rivalry also beset the shores of the North Sea and the Baltic. Hamburg, Bremen, Lübeck and other wealthy cities had banded together to form the Hanseatic League. They were not content to assist each other in their far-flung commerce; they also maintained a crack army and a first-rate navy which discouraged outside predators and protected the northern waterways. The Hansa cities had to contend with the ambitions of Sweden and Denmark, which were then in their heyday as vigorous aggressive powers.

To complicate matters further, the whole feeble structure of European states was, at the moment, shaking under the battering ram of the Ottoman Turkish war machine. After subduing large parts of western Asia and North Africa, Sultan Suleiman the Magnificent had extended his empire over the whole Balkan Peninsula. He had conquered Hungary and had advanced deep into Austria. Though he professed the faith of Muhammad, the Prophet of Allah, he was aided and encouraged by some Christian rulers who saw in him an instrument to subdue their Christian rivals. Those were the morals of power politics.

Eagerly Ivan absorbed the rules and the techniques of the power game. It was a game to which he had not yet been invited. Nobody, beyond the great eastern plains, paid any attention to Moscow. If it was thought of at all, it was considered the frozen abode of crude barbarians who amounted to nothing. It was best to leave them to their bear hunts and their drinking bouts.

The Czar decided to seek access to the international chess board. Russia had to demand a place in the tournament in which the pawns were provinces and cities full of people, fields heavy with crops and traffic ways carrying the wealth created by human hands.

It is highly doubtful that Ivan could have read *The Prince*, by Niccolò Machiavelli, the great Italian humanist, who died three years before the Rurik prince was born. But whether he heard about him or developed the idea independently, he became a master in the Machiavellian type of ruthless power politics which knows only one valid measuring stick of human conduct—success.

With all his talent and impatient drive, Ivan threw himself into the game. Soon the courts of Europe began to take notice. Delegations shuttled between Moscow and foreign capitals. Embassies were sent and received. The tricks of the trade included secret concessions and alliances, bribery of officials, false promises, open and veiled threats. These tools of high diplomacy had been perfected at the courts of Constantinople and Paris, of Madrid and of the Holy See. Now they were tried within the gates of the Kremlin. Ivan quickly learned to speak the language of diplomacy, with its eternal unctuous references to the deity. Observing how Protestants, Catholics and Muslims, whether fighting one another or betraying the members of their own faith, constantly pretended to have God on their side, he found it easy to fall into step.

Ivan Vasilievich became a master diplomat of the European Renaissance model, but he conducted affairs of state in typical Russian style. Lavish display had to cover up the feeling of inferiority. Eternal suspicion and a preoccupation with minute details marred the over-all performance of Russian officials in the sixteenth century, as it still does to a large extent today.

Embassies setting out for the Austrian or the Polish capital traveled with five hundred richly arrayed horses which were loaded with overwhelmingly generous gifts. Delegates from foreign courts had to be extremely careful lest they offend the Czar by some inadvertent slight. Their period of waiting for a royal audience depended on the importance of the governments they represented. Written messages from crowned heads had to be sealed with the great seal of the sovereign and be presented by a personage of sufficiently high standing. Otherwise the visitors faced quick dismissal from the royal presence.

Foreign embassies were kept from any contact with the people. Along their route of travel, villages were evacuated, especially when they had suffered from famine or from recent hostile raids. When more than one ambassador happened to be in Moscow at the same time, they were so closely guarded that one did not even know of the other's presence, enabling the Czar to negotiate with each without the other's knowledge.

Calculated design and almost childish pettiness mingled in the treatment of official visitors. To impress them properly, the schedule of activities always included a tour of the heavily guarded chambers beneath the Kremlin which housed the Czar's unrivaled collection of gold objects and precious gems. When giving audiences to ambassadors who were not of the Orthodox faith, Ivan had a basin of water ready by his side so he could wash away the impurity caused by touching an infidel.

While the foreigners bridled at some of the calculated arrogance they had to put up with, they were astonished by the abject humility displayed in religious rites. On Palm Sunday they witnessed a procession in which the Metropolitan rode sideways on a horse equipped with artificial ears to simulate the ass which had borne Christ into Jerusalem. The autocratic ruler in person walked in the dust, leading the horse by its bridle.

Another ceremony which startled the assembled ambassadors was the blessing of the waters. Court and clergy holding crosses and banners walked upon the ice of the Moskva River. A hole was punched in the ice. A cup of river water was blessed with chanting and censing and then poured over the Czar. After lesser notables had been likewise soaked with the blessed water, men, women and children stripped naked to jump into the ice-rimmed hole.

Back in his chambers, where he closeted himself with top

advisers and reexamined the map of Europe, Ivan understood fully that two main obstacles prevented him from becoming a full partner in the club of continental politics. First, Russia was greatly hampered in her direct communication with the more advanced countries because two hostile powers blocked access on her western flank. These were Poland and Lithuania. They have long since been reduced to relative unimportance, but in the sixteenth century their armies commanded considerable respect.

Secondly, what troubled the Czar even more was that his realm lacked an outlet to the sea. It was an immense mass of tundra, forest and steppe, but completely landlocked, except for the frozen Arctic. There by the mouth of the Dvina, his friends, the indomitable Britishers, had established a trading station and named it Archangel after the angel St. Michael. But this port was open only three months of the year.

All the more developed countries were sea powers. In order to catch up with them, Russia needed ports from which Russian ships could venture into the open ocean. It needed outlets to the Baltic Sea in the north and to the Mediterranean by way of the Black Sea in the south. Ever since the days of Ivan, czars and Communist commissars alike have pursued the same goals.

Prudently Ivan ruled out the possibility of winning access to the Black Sea during his reign. There sat the Turkish lion growling at anybody who would dare to approach. The Czar was not about to tweak its tail. The animal was dangerous, and its fangs were strong and deadly. Such an undertaking had to wait until future centuries, when the royal beast became old and decrepit.

But the Baltic coast was quite another matter. It was closer at hand, and no superpower guarded it with an invincible military machine.

Under bushy eyebrows, the greedy eyes of the royal strategist scanned the map. His writing quill, heavy with black ink, hovered over a patch heavily marked with such names as Narva, Dorpat and Reval. The quill plunged down, leaving a strong cross-sign which covered these names of bustling ice-free port cities. Often they were shrouded in wet fog, and the winter sun visited them only briefly, but they were snugly protected from the killing frosts of the Arctic. From there ships plied the inland sea to Sweden, Denmark and the Hansa cities, bringing their owners fat profits and high standing in the council chambers of the cities.

This stretch of heath and sand dunes was Livonia. There is no use trying to look up the name in an atlas unless it is a historical one, for this awkward political monstrosity has long ceased to exist. Prussia, Latvia and Esthonia were later to plant their flags on the towns and villages of the province, but now the flags are gone, and the powers for which they stood inhabit the graveyard of history.

In Ivan's time, Livonia was nominally part of the Holy Roman Empire, but the emperor, a staunch Catholic, was far away and had his hands full with the aggressive Turks and with Protestant rebels closer to home. He had never even been near that area, which was populated mostly by Slavs, many of whom spoke Russian and adhered to the Orthodox faith.

Closer to home, the official task of ruling Livonia was vested in the Teutonic Knights, who by the sixteenth century had completely outlived their reason for existence. They were as anachronistic as the chariot would be in the days of the sportscar. In the Middle Ages, the Teutonic Knights, an order of German fighting monks, were entrusted with the task of defending the holy shrines of Christianity, which had been wrested from Muslim hands during the First Crusade. Later the Holy Land fell to the Muslims once more. There was nothing left to defend for the various orders of Christian knights. They had to look around for other places where they could apply their fighting valor, and so the Teutonic Knights moved to the Baltic, conquered the land and converted the pagan Slavs by the sword.

Now the order had lost its vigor. The knights indulged in soft living and in unmonastic luxury. Livonia had dissolved into a loose combination of semi-independent cities and bishoprics. German Protestants had moved in and formed an important middle-class element.

Ivan's efficient spies filled him in on all the dreary details. Livonia was a rotten tree ready for the brawny logger's ax. Land-hungry rulers are never at a loss to find excuses for aggression. Ivan claimed that the whole area once belonged to his Rurik ancestors. Therefore Livonians were forever to be regarded as his subjects. He proclaimed self-righteously, "The maritime lands of our fathers and grandfathers on the Baltic Sea have been rent from our soil. I owe it to my glorious ancestors to recover them."

His emissaries demanded the payment of tribute as a token of submission. The worried Livonians sent delegates, but no money. "If you don't bring the tribute speedily," the incensed Czar shouted at them, "we shall find means to come and take it."

The Livonians stalled for time. They made promises while the helpless Teutonic Knights frantically sought assistance from Danes, Swedes and Poles. Catholic and Protestant princes promised help, but no deeds backed up the words.

The time for action arrived. Ivan summoned Prince Andrei Kurbsky, one of the few men he trusted completely. Kurbsky was slightly older than his sovereign. A descendant of an illustrious, once independent princely family, he had distinguished himself at the conquest of Kazan. His keen intelligence matched that of the Czar, who esteemed him highly. "Andrei, my friend, the Livonians are suppressing our Russian brothers," he was told. "They have despoiled our Orthodox churches and desecrated the holy icons. Go and punish them. Restore to us their lands. The Holy Mother will protect you."

Kurbsky went forth with a motley army of boyars, Cossacks and a large contingent of loyal Tatars. German and Dutch gunners accompanied them.

The fields were damp and green, the marshes alive with wild-fowl when the double-headed eagle was carried into Livonia. No army stood guard by the lazily winding rivers. It was less a war than a methodical ravaging of the countryside. Villages were burned, peasants slain and their women captured for the pleasure of the troops. One Tatar commander accidentally strayed into Russian territory, where his men administered to loyal subjects of the Czar the same kind of treatment. He was severely reprimanded and ordered to make restitutions.

Hardly any resistance was encountered until the Russians reached the city of Narva. There they had to settle down for a lengthy siege, which was directed from a stronghold across the estuary of the Narva River. Kurbsky had ordered it built by hastily conscripted peasants from the neighboring villages. This military camp was named Ivangorod, the city of Ivan.

Food became scarce in Narva, but its merchants and craftsmen refused to surrender, hoping for the reinforcements which the Grand Master of the Teutonic Order had promised. They never came. One night fire broke out inside the walls. From their bivouacs in Ivangorod, Russian soldiers saw the flames reddening the sky. Without waiting for orders, they piled into boats. Some, eager to get there in time for the fun, paddled across the estuary on unhinged doors. Seeing their hands forced, the commanders ordered the bugles blown for a general attack. When the first rays of the sun tried to break through the fog and smoke, the double-eagle flew from the roof of the town hall. Moscow greeted the news with joyous feasting in the cathedrals and in the streets.

The cities of Northern Livonia sued for an armistice. By 1558 Ivan had won his "window to the Baltic" and with it his seat at the conference table of the top-ranking European powers, who were now his nextdoor neighbors.

Several merchant ships were found at anchor in the conquered ports. With the black flag of the Ruriks fluttering from their masts and skippered by foreign seamen, they nosed their way into the Baltic Sea. Russia had acquired its first fleet.

After the signing of the armistice, normal life began to return to the Livonian cities. Ivan recognized their economic value, and he encouraged their German burghers to reopen shops and counting houses. They were allowed to maintain their Protestant churches, except for those that had previously been converted from Orthodox houses of worship.

On his visits the Czar indulged in his favorite pastime of religious disputation whenever he ran into a Protestant theologian. The arguments remained friendly unless he happened to lose his temper. Once a Lutheran pastor angered him with some quotations from the great reformer. "The devil take your Luther," shouted the mounted monarch, slashing the minister's face with his whip and riding off. Arguing about religion with the champion of Orthodox Christianity could be a risky business.

With his new port cities secure, Ivan could focus his attention on trouble spots in the south and east. Russia was growing in size, but its heartland was still far from danger free. Though vanquished in open battle, large Tatar bands had never submitted to the house of Rurik. They kept on roaming the steppes, elusive and quick to swoop down upon weaker prey and carry off what they could lift onto their swift horses. Merchant caravans and isolated cities were their favorite targets.

Kazan had been conquered, but it took five more years of costly fighting to clear the surrounding land of highly mobile bands determined on vengeance and loot. That eliminated one source of trouble, but another problem still remained—the khanate of the Crimea. Its squadrons at times raided perilously close to the gates of Moscow. But when organized Russian forces went after them, they quickly withdrew to their sanctuary under the cover of the Turkish Sultan's large umbrella.

Keeping a wary eye on the Tatar scene, Ivan skillfully deployed his newly acquired diplomatic skill. His agents turned one Tatar princeling against the other, promising gold, land or well-paid positions in the Russian officers' corps. Christian rulers were forever trying to draw the Czar into a holy alliance against

the Turks. He refused putting self-preservation above Christian
solidarity despite his personal near-fanatic piety. When his troops
occasionally captured Turkish advisers or even soldiers fighting
alongside the Tatars, he always sent them back to the Sultan with
his compliments.

Although Ivan realized that a march to the Black Sea was premature, the conquest of the lower Volga valley from the Crimean
khan was within reach. This would bring the longest European
waterway completely into Russian hands.

The Volga opens into a wide delta and eventually disappears
in the salty Caspian Sea, which is not a sea at all, but the largest
lake in the world. At the head of the delta, dominating the access
to the Caspian, lies the city of Astrakhan, famed for its caviar and
its fur made from the skins of newborn lambs.

The double-eagle was poised for a flight to the mosques of
Astrakhan. It reached its destination swiftly.

While rival factions, cheered on by Russian emissaries, kept
the city in disarray, an army of three hundred thousand men
approached on land and in riverboats. At the news, the khan fled
in such haste that his harem, consisting of four wives and
numerous concubines, was left behind. The marvelously rich
booty included sixty thousand horses, among them two hundred
thoroughbreds which were brought back to grace and to improve
the quality of the royal stables.

Astrakhan, the last important Tatar stronghold in Europe, fell
with hardly a drop of blood spilled. A subservient Tatar puppet
was set up, and he promised to pay a yearly tribute of three
thousand caviar-producing sturgeon in addition to a large quan-
tity of gold pieces. The Volga was now a Russian highway, and
its crossings could become the staging points for even more
ambitious expeditions to the mysterious east.

The *Te Deum* was chanted in the newly completed cathedral
of St. Basil, symbol of triumph and promise of future greatness.

The window to the Baltic was open. The Tatars were on the

run. Pope, Emperor, Sultan, princes big and small began to look with amazement and with fear at the eastern giant, dormant so long and now beginning to stir.

In the prime of his manhood, the Czar had reached the summit. The future looked bright, not only on the political horizon but also in the privacy of his family. Still at his side was Anastasia, the beloved "little heifer," always submissive, yet exerting a soothing influence on her husband's volcanic temper. In 1554 she had borne him another son, Ivan Ivanovich. In contrast to little Dmitri, this boy was sturdy and in the best of health. The royal line had an heir. The succession seemed secure.

With relish the Czar drank in the love and admiration poured out to him by his people. Worshipfully they began to call him by a new name: Ivan Grozni. The Russian word *grozni* means awe-inspiring or fearsome, as the Lord Himself may be called fearsome by the faithful. It was only later that *grozni* came to be translated as "terrible," in the sense of one who strikes terror in the hearts of men by his atrocious deeds.

9
DARKNESS

In summertime, the sun is bright and warm over the fields and pastures around Moscow. Under the azure sky, the high stalks of yellow grain wave lazily in the light breeze. Red poppies and blue cornflowers add to the symphony of colors, and next to them the freshly turned black earth is fragrant with the scent of strength and fertility.

But there come days when suddenly the sun disappears behind black clouds. A growling thunderstorm rushes in. The sky bursts into torrents of rain or hail. The earth seems to drown, and the colors are swallowed up in a monotonous world of ugly gray. Sadly the peasant looks at the destruction of what he had built through many months of toil.

For thirteen years, Anastasia had been the ideal wife, modest and retiring, keeping to her quarters in the company of her ladies-in-waiting and a few page boys, none over ten years old. When she appeared in public, she came to relieve suffering. After every victory she obtained the release of many prisoners. The people loved her.

Now Anastasia was ailing. While most Russian women were of robust build, she was frail, a delicate flower in need of tender care. She had borne her husband six children, among them Ivan, the Czarevich, and Feodor, who, as everybody could see, was mentally handicapped like his uncle Yuri. Like so many other royal families, the Ruriks had their share of defective offspring.

Four children had died in infancy, a not uncommon fate in those days, when babies were left tightly swaddled with no room to move, not even to breathe properly. All this had left Anastasia weakened. When Ivan finally became aware of his wife's poor physical condition, he prescribed his favorite treatment—pilgrimages to distant monasteries, where they prayed in musty chapels before icons darkened by the smoke of flickering candles.

Those travels would have been an ordeal for the sturdiest creature; they were poison for this fragile woman. In November, 1559, returning from the monastery at Mozhaisk, she became seriously ill. No medicine was at hand, not even a sled to transport the patient in some degree of comfort. Her cheeks were an unhealthy feverish red as she sat up in the rumbling conveyance during the painful return trip.

Anastasia was never to leave her sickchamber alive. Her pale skin became almost translucent. The eyes appeared enormously big in the shrunken face, but they retained their expression of warmth and compassionate modesty. The doctors shook their heads in frustration and tried to avert the searching eyes of the disconsolate husband. "Bring monks," shouted the frantic Czar, "bring magicians, sorcerers, bring anybody who might save my little heifer."

They came, whole squads of them. They chanted, they brought holy relics, they drew mysterious circles and sprinkled foulsmelling liquids and powders over the bedside. It was of no avail.

In the following summer, the Czar, broken in spirit, his hair disheveled, his clothes torn, walked behind the coffin as it was carried to its resting place. By the thousands the simple folk lined the roads. Their tears were sincere. Somehow they felt that with the death of the gentle Czarina a light had been snuffed out and darkness lay ahead.

Ivan never recovered from the blow. He made rich donations to monasteries as far away as Greece so that the monks would pray for the repose of Anastasia's soul, but in his own tortured soul all the demonic forces which had lain dormant now came to the fore.

He kept to himself, brooding, indulging in extreme self-pity. It was then that he took on the appearance often displayed in Russian paintings: a tall haggard man with a shaggy, prematurely gray beard, a sharp nose and eyes peering in hostility from under a heavily creased forehead.

Anastasia was the only person whom he had really loved. Nobody was ever to take her place. Why had she been taken from him? Suspicion, the old curse of his childhood, crept again into his conscious mind. It gave him a ready explanation: poison.

And the culprits? Of course, the boyars—plotters and traitors all of them. Like an old wound with the scab suddenly torn away, the hatred of those proud nobles broke out again, those princes who had never been reconciled to the loss of their quasi-independent positions.

He took to carrying a long and heavy metal-tipped staff at all times with which he lashed out in sudden fury at anyone within reach. Aides and servants learned to scuttle to a safe distance whenever the first signs of wrath appeared.

During his own illness, the monarch had become disillusioned with his chief advisers. Now, shaking off all restraints, he proceeded to get rid of them. Adashev was dispatched to govern a conquered city in Livonia. Later an order was sent for his arrest, but he died before it could be carried out. Sylvester, the priest, disappeared to a solitary monastery on the far northern coast.

The monk Maxim the Greek had once advised the Czar, "Don't keep men about you who are your equals or who are superior to you in intelligence." He remembered, and from then on his retinue became a group of yes-men, fawning and flattering and always making sure to keep away from the dreaded staff.

Drunkenness and debauchery became a daily routine. He indulged his sexual urges freely. Women were objects to be used and discarded. Scouts searched the land for desirable females, single or married to respectable citizens. The royal court became a harem, like the residence of an oriental potentate. Once the women had satisfied Ivan's fancy, they were returned to their husbands or passed on to some court favorites.

But those extramarital diversions did not diminish the growing demand for a second marriage. It was the old problem of succession. The Czarevich was a child. The more legitimate male offspring were produced, the more secure the crown would rest on the head of the Rurik prince. Nobody could replace Anastasia, and so it was without any deep feelings that the Czar became a bridegroom again only three months after the death of his "little heifer." In choosing a spouse he played a cruel joke on the detested boyars. If any of them had hoped for a second chance to become in-laws to royalty, they saw their dreams shattered when he selected a Circassian princess, the daughter of a Muslim khan. Baptized under the name of Maria, she aroused Ivan's passion for a while, but no deeper emotional relationship developed. In character, background and behavior, she was the very opposite of Anastasia.

It seemed that the change in the ruler's life had affected the whole country. The dream of a mighty unified empire faded into the distance. What had been tied together with much toil and patience threatened to come apart.

The murky clouds over the Baltic thickened. The Russian position in Livonia appeared shaky despite the stunning victories —or, rather, because of them. The little semibarbaric principality of Moscow had been of small concern to her western neighbors, but as they faced an expanding Russian empire they became alarmed. Swedish and Danish emissaries scuttled around the continent looking for possible allies. Even more concerned was the country which shut off Russia almost completely from intercourse with the West. This was Lithuania, a sizable kingdom at the time, stretching along the Czar's domain all the way from the Baltic to the Crimea.

The Lithuanian subjects were mostly Slavic people, White Russians and Ukrainians, ethnic cousins of Ivan's own Great Russians. The majority practiced the Eastern Orthodox form of Christianity exactly like the Muscovites. Kiev, scene of the Rurik family's first glory, was now a Lithuanian city, but it was still coveted by the princes of Moscow, who considered it their legitimate possession. Ivan would have liked nothing better than to ride triumphantly into Kiev, but this was definitely not the time to attempt the march.

Though the Lithuanians resembled the Russians in many aspects, they did not cherish the idea of being exposed to the moods and the long staff of the man in the Kremlin. Least of all was this the wish of the Jagellonian dynasty which ruled Lithuania. They had no desire to commit political suicide.

To discourage any designs of her voracious Russian neighbor, Lithuania formed a strong alliance with Poland, the land on its western border, then in its period of greatest vigor. Ever since the fourteenth century, the kings of Lithuania had doubled as Poland's monarchs, though otherwise the administration of the two countries remained separate. But in 1569 they were officially unified under King Sigismund. This step was a clear warning that there was a limit to Ivan's appetite.

Moscow bristled over the many pin pricks of calculated Polish-Lithuanian hostility. All through traffic from western Europe was shut off by the dual monarchy. Much-needed weaponry bought in Germany and Holland could not pass into Russia. Cannoniers, technicians and mercenary soldiers hired in the West to fight under the double-eagle were turned back at the Polish-Russian border.

The enemy even tried to pressure the Queen of England into stopping trade with Russia. Sigismund wrote to Elizabeth:

We perfectly know Your Majesty cannot be ignorant how great the cruelty is of the said enemy, of what force he is, what tyranny he uses on his subjects, and in what servile sort they be under him. Therefore we that know best, and border upon him, do admonish other Christian princes in time that they do not betray their dignity, liberty and life of them and their subjects to a most barbarous and cruel enemy.

The letter did not mention that cruelty in Poland was hardly of a lesser variety than that in Russia. Anyhow, the queen's answer was polite and noncommital. She was not about to pass up a good bargain just to please distant Christian princes whom she saw no reason to favor. And so British merchandise continued to trickle through the ice-shrouded port of Archangel.

Ivan saw confrontation looming, and he disliked the prospect. While conquest of Lithuania fitted into his masterplan of a Greater Russia, he wanted to avoid open conflict with the Poles, who were Catholics and strongly oriented towards western European culture. Poles would consider war against Orthodox Russians a religious crusade and fight with stubborn fanaticism. In addition, their foot soldiers were well drilled and disciplined mercenaries, and the squadrons of the Polish cavalry were vastly superior to their Russian counterparts. They moved and regrouped with ease, whereas the Russians usually spent their whole energy and courage in the initial assault.

Knowing all this, Ivan tried diplomacy. But even in this game, which he usually played to perfection, his performance was now, to say the least, uneven. To pacify at least one of the several potential enemies, he made the brother of the Danish king the puppet ruler of captured Livonia. But the puppet deserted when the going got rough.

Delegations with secret messages shuttled between Moscow and Cracow, the Polish capital. One Russian emissary brought a proposal of marriage between the Czar and King Sigismund's sister Catherine. That Ivan already had a wife at the time did not seem to matter; there were plenty of nunneries in Russia. Instead of his sister, the Polish king sent a white mare as a suitable mate. In response, Ivan had a big hole dug to await the Polish king's body whenever it would come into his hands. These were the niceties of diplomatic dealings.

Smarting under Sigismund's calculated insult, Ivan turned to interfering in the muddled internal politics of Poland. He subsidized nobles to rise against their king, and when Sigismund died, he presented himself as a candidate for the Polish crown. Traditionally the aristocracy elected the ruler either from the Polish nobility or from outside the country. This invited endless schemes of bribery, lobbying and outside pressure and eventually contributed to the downfall of the country.

The Czar of Russia as King of Poland: that would indeed have been a switch. It would have drastically altered the course of history; but it was not to be. Despite the gold and the ample promises arriving from Moscow, the majority of votes was cast for Stephen Batory, a little-known Hungarian nobleman.

The Polish gentry wished to elect a nobody who would leave them to their own devices, but this time they had made a mistake. Stephen Batory turned out to be a most able ruler and a particularly gifted military leader. Soon he focused his attention on Russia. If Poland was to survive as an independent power, Moscow had to be stopped.

Russian forces had been ravaging northern Livonia at will. Under force, its cities had already sworn allegiance to the Czar. There was no doubt that he intended to swallow up the rest of this unhappy region as well. The Grand Master of the near impotent Teutonic Knights was still frantically casting about for help. Only Poland, feeling herself threatened, responded, with some feeble assistance contributed by Sweden.

A nasty war began between Russians and Poles which was to last for twenty-four years, almost to the end of Ivan's reign, costly in lives and in destroyed resources. Its result was century-long bitterness between the two Slavic nations.

Polish armies advanced against Russian positions, and things went badly for the Czar's forces. They became quickly discouraged. Officers still tended to act independently of one another. The Tatar auxiliaries especially insisted on playing the game in their own way. Money to pay the soldiers became scarce. Peasants had to be recruited by force to dig earthworks for fortifications. During the night they would run away in droves.

No military man himself, Ivan sent his generals to conduct the war while he waited at various monasteries for their reports. There were some victories, such as the capture of Polotzk, an important Lithuanian city, but more frequent was the news of defeats and retreats. Instinctively he blamed them on treason. Many boyars had relatives in Lithuania. Whom could he trust?

A message came, and it struck a blow almost as staggering as the loss of Anastasia. Andrei Kurbsky, his close friend of many years, had fought a battle against the Poles and lost. But this was not the worst of the news. Fearing the Czar's well-known wrath, Kurbsky had defected to the enemy in the dead of the night.

It turned out to have been a well-prepared act. Two horses were waiting for the commander as he sneaked out of the camp. At the nearest Polish encampment he was received with jubilation. The king, hardly concealing his glee, showered honors upon Kurbsky and granted him large estates and castles. Other boyars followed. Loudly the voices of aristocratic Russian émigrés called for the chastisement of the terrible Czar who was so hard on their own social class.

Kurbsky's defection had a bizarre aftermath. Under the white flag of truce, an emissary crossed the battle line. He was brought into the Czar's presence. Standing stiff without making the required prostration, he handed over a letter from the defector. A glimmer of satisfaction shone in Ivan's eyes. Surely the former favorite now had second thoughts about his betrayal.

Eagerly the Czar began to read. After scanning the first sentences, his face darkened. Seeing the telltale signs of an impending outburst, the servants retreated to a safe distance. Not so the letter carrier. Foaming at the mouth with rage, Ivan raised his staff and stabbed at the foot of the man in front of him. The sharp point went through the flesh and nailed it to the wooden floor. "Here," shouted the Czar, "you read to me the message of your infamous master."

He threw the letter at Kurbsky's faithful servant, who, suppressing the seering pain, read it aloud. It was not a plea for forgiveness, but a violent dressing-down, a recital of royal sins couched in numerous references to God and the Bible.

To a once serene majesty, made famous by God, but now darkened by your sins, by the infernal hate in your heart, diseased in conscience. To the tyrant, unexampled among the most unfaithful lords of the world.

This was only the introduction. A long list of accusations followed, replete with threats of divine punishment and appeals to the saints for intercession.

Dost thou think thou art immortal? Is there not a God and a court of judgment of the Highest upon a czar? In my confusion of heart I cannot say all the wrong thou hast done me. I will say but one thing: thou has deprived me of holy Russia.

Here spoke the foremost boyar, lashing out vigorously at Ivan's habit of relying on members of the lower classes:

You choose your clerks not from noble and highborn stock, but rather from priests' sons and from the rank and file.

What was even more astounding than Kurbsky's effrontery was Ivan's answer. He wrote a lengthy epistle chastising the defector and defending his own position. Several more such letters were exchanged. Kurbsky wrote five, and the Czar sent two in which he called his former friend "vicious dog" and "cowardly traitor" and declared, "Your counsel stinks worse than dung."

One of Ivan's dispatches extended over sixty pages and revealed not only his political stand, but the whole state of his troubled mind. The man who was convinced of his divine mandate to rule without any restriction still found it necessary, again and again, to justify himself, even to a hated enemy. He needed to cry out to the world the tragedy of his life, the loneliness of his existence:

You and all your evil deeds are to blame. For you and the priest [Sylvester] had decided that I shall be czar in name only while you and the priest will govern. . . . You are the servant of those enemies of Christianity who have apostacized from the worship of divine icons and befouled and trampled our sacred vessels and images. . . . Why did you divide me from my wife? Had you not taken from me my young heifer? In vain I have looked for some man to have pity on me, but I have found none.

Anastasia had died years before, and Kurbsky could hardly have had anything to do with it. But now, in Ivan's agony, all tragic events seemed somehow linked, and they appeared to him as a single giant conspiracy to rob him of his happiness, of his throne, of his life. Had psychiatrists existed in those days, they would have diagnosed a dangerous persecution complex, dangerous to the patient and dangerous to those over whom he exercised power.

From the letters of the two antagonists, dictated by the violent emotions of hate, disappointment and frustration, we can reconstruct the make-up of two personalities, children of the same century, sharing language and nationality, yet different in almost everything else. Kurbsky represented the conservatism of the old privileged group. He abhorred any change in the social structure of Russia. Rank and family precedence were for him sacred privileges, and any attempt to tamper with them was an offense against the Almighty Himself. To him the concept of a powerful and united Russia meant nothing; the status of his class, the high nobility, meant everything. In the interest of his feudal role he even turned against his own nation. Perhaps he felt remorse for what he had done, but he covered such feelings by ever-increasing attacks against his former sovereign.

On the opposite side, beyond the battlefields, brooded the Czar, at heart an innovator and possessed of an exploring intellect, searching for new, progressive ways, yet confused and uncertain about the directions in which to move. Before his piercing eyes was the vague image of a modern state, a nation resting on a broad base of popular support, but represented by and symbolized in a single exalted leading figure. At every step he took to reach this shining goal, lack of knowledge, of training and of reliable, capable helpers blocked his way. These were his occupational predicaments, which were compounded by the pitiful state of his emotions. His heart cried out, yearning to be loved, yet he found himself betrayed and forsaken, his trust rejected, his feeling of security vanished. Added to the grief over Anastasia's passing, Kurbsky's desertion left a lingering poison in the sovereign's soul, a poison for which there was no antidote.

The unique correspondence between a ruler and his former aide who had betrayed him is of interest not only to the student of human emotions. It has become a most important set of documents concerning the history of a time and place for which contemporary source material is extremely rare.

Kurbsky never returned to his homeland, but apparently he could not get Russia or its ruler out of his mind. Long after the exchange of letters had ceased, he composed a history of Ivan's reign. Like his letters, this work is extremely biased. Its pages are filled with bitter recriminations and with constant assurances that his own cause was just and in line with God's will. But even with all their limitations, these sources help us to gain some understanding of the man whom Kurbsky defamed and whose ideal of divinely ordained monarchy he abhorred.

10
BLACK TERROR

Something was up. The word spread through the crooked streets, from house to house, from shop to shop. Early on that December morning in 1564, Muscovites left their warm stoves and streamed towards Red Square. The longer they watched the strange proceedings, the more bewildered they became. What did it all mean?

Before the Kremlin gate was drawn up a line of sleighs. Teams of sturdy draft horses impatiently stomped the packed snow, their nostrils emitting clouds of vapor. Despite the intense cold, servants perspired under their fur cloaks as they loaded huge chests onto the sleighs. The Czar's furniture, icons, the gold-plated chinaware and even his collections of coins and weapons were carried out.

Several hundred mounted guardsmen with heavy saddle packs took up positions around the convoy of sleighs. The Czar himself appeared wrapped in sable and ermine so that only his eyes and beard were visible. There were some jeers from the back rows of the onlookers as the new Czarina was conducted to her sleigh. She was rumored to be a woman of loose morals, as much disliked as Anastasia had been loved.

At the sound of trumpets, the whole train lurched into motion.

The sleigh horses began to pull under protest, while the cavalry mounts pranced impatiently around them. Slowly they crossed the thick ice of the Moskva and disappeared into the endless whiteness of the winterscape.

Left behind on the square, the people were worried. This was not one of the usual sorties. It could hardly be another bear hunt or pilgrimage. It looked as if the ruler was moving away for good.

The following days witnessed a growth of general anxiety. "What will become of us?" asked the clerks, the merchants and the craftsmen. The stalls were deserted. The whole machinery of government seemed to grind to a halt.

This deep concern was proof that Ivan was still popular despite his fits of cruelty. He was the symbol of strength and unity, the transmitter of divine grace. Without him, chaos was imminent.

For a whole month there was no news of the Czar's whereabouts. Then came two letters sent from the village of Alexandrov, about one hundred miles from the capital. One was addressed to the Metropolitan:

We are abdicating the throne of our fathers. Not wishing to endure any longer the treachery of the boyars and of many clergymen, we with great pity in our hearts, have quitted the Czardom and have gone wherever God may lead us.

The second communication was to the "merchants and people of Moscow." In even stronger terms it reiterated the evil deeds of the nobility and clergy which made it impossible for the monarch to rule properly. "But I do not bear you ill will," it concluded. "I know your love for us, and I will always return it manyfold."

With his considerable theatrical talent, Ivan had again staged a cleverly designed drama. Great risks were involved, but the stakes were high.

He had, of course, never intended to give up his rule. Pulling strings from Alexandrov, he made sure that the second letter was read publicly on Red Square, and the effect was exactly what he had expected. There was general sobbing and wailing, for the Slavic mentality does not shrink from the open display of emotions.

The mood of the masses was ugly, and wisely the frightened boyars kept at a safe distance.

"We must go to the Czar," the people shouted. "We must beg him to return."

"Death to all who cause him sorrow. Let him punish his enemies as he sees fit."

Standing on a wooden crate, an unknown wool trader summed up the general feeling: "Let the Czar execute the wrongdoers. In life and death his will is supreme. The Czardom cannot remain without its head."

Hurriedly a delegation was formed and dispatched to Alexandrov. It was composed of the most prominent merchants and some reluctant boyars and churchmen. In a day and a half they covered the distance which had taken the Czar's party almost three weeks.

Admitted to the emperor's presence, they were shocked by his appearance. His face was gray and drawn, his hair had become sparse. Before them stood a man beset by deep inner struggles and doubts.

Still, he could play his role to perfection, as they found out as soon as the actual negotiations got under way. Yes, he might consider returning, but only on his own terms. Topping the list of terms was an absolutely free hand in restructuring the government machinery and in weeding out any person not to his liking. The delegation was in no position to argue. It did not take much imagination to figure out what fate awaited them should they return unsuccessful.

The play moved into its second act, and the director handled it with consummate skill, squeezing from the script the last ounce of suspense. He did not rush to Moscow immediately. The longer the people had to wait, the more receptive would they be to what he had in mind.

Finally, in February, 1565, the long cortege wound its way back the same route it had come a few months before. In the streets of Moscow, the people were kneeling in the snow, reaching out to kiss his hands, the fringes of his garments, even his boots and stirrups. The Little Father was back; now everything would be all right.

It did not take long for the country to find out what the Little Father meant to do with his free hand.

One impatient gesture shoved aside the Council of Boyars, the old aristocratic decision-making body. In its place a representative assembly, the *Zemski Sobor,* was called. It was not democratically elected by any means, but it did, for the first time, contain merchants and tradesmen among its delegates. The debates were free and often quite heated, but in the end, the Czar's proposals were regularly adopted with overwhelming support.

Then, still overly concerned with his personal safety, the monarch created a new bodyguard of one thousand hand-picked men, the *oprichniky.* Belonging to the landless nobility or even to lesser social strata, their main qualification was unconditional and unswerving loyalty to the person of the Czar. With blood-curdling oaths they bound themselves in a tight brotherhood, pledging to make no friendship outside their circle and not to let love of parents or relatives interfere with allegiance to their master.

Eventually the ranks of the *oprichniky* swelled to some six thousand, mostly young daredevils, including a number of foreigners. One of those was Heinrich von Staden, an unscrupulous German adventurer who later skipped the country and ingratiated himself with Ivan's enemies by publishing damaging reports about the Czar.

In a matter of months, the *oprichniky* aroused a general dread like that of the devil himself. They rode black horses and wore black gowns and hats, and on their saddles they displayed a dog's head as a symbol of ferocity and a broom-shaped whip to sweep away all resistance to the crown.

They fell upon their victims, killing and maiming mercilessly. Neither rank nor ancestry was any protection from their fury. Provincial governors, generals and churchmen shivered at the mention of the black troopers. Plunder and rape were on their daily agenda.

With a bold stroke which has been termed a revolution from above, Ivan completely overturned the country's administration in order to break, once and for all, the stranglehold of the petty princes and large landholders. The country was divided into halves, not along a continuous line, but by assigning diverse territories to one or the other segment. One half was turned over to the *oprichniky,* which meant that the Czar administered it without regard to older privileges or institutions. There his will was the only law; the black riders were the only enforcers.

In the other half, the *zemshchina,* the old officials, remained. They were mainly boyars, generally the only group with some sort of experience in handling governmental business.

Moscow itself was split in two. The section assigned to the *oprichniky* was cleared of all other inhabitants whatever their rank or station. They had to vacate immediately without their possessions. The same went on all over the country. In the bitter cold winter of 1565, some 12,000 landholders and their families were forced to leave their homes, many on foot.

The evicted were officially compensated with other lands, but when they arrived there, often after traveling enormous distances, they found themselves in virgin land without shelter.

The result was a thorough reshuffling of the population. The nobility was not abolished, but it lost its links with ancestral

homes and with old tenants. Ties of blood and bonds of neighborhood were broken, and the traditional centers of resistance wiped
out.

All settlements and castles which lay along the main lines of
communication or on important crossroads fell to the *oprichniky*.
This revolution from above seemed to deliberately create chaos,
yet it made sense in the context of turning the loose territories
into a unified state.

There is more than a casual resemblance between the *oprichniky* and the notorious secret police which did its bloody work
under Stalin's regime. The SS guards of Adolf Hitler were also
akin to Ivan's dreaded private army.

When atrocities are not only officially sanctioned but even
encouraged and rewarded, they become a way of life. The tales
of the horrors perpetrated by the riders with the dog's heads make
grim reading, though we must remember that the *oprichniky* had
no monopoly on cruelty. The highly placed in Russia had practiced it all along on their inferiors. What was new was that the
highly placed were now given the same treatment.

Nor were barbaric acts restricted to Russia. They had their
counterparts in the massacres of rebellious German peasants, in
the extermination of the Anabaptists and in the proceedings of
the Spanish Inquisition.

Some reports, such as Kurbsky's highly prejudiced history,
were undoubtedly exaggerated. But even when we discount much
of it, what remains is still a sad indictment of man's inhumanity
towards his fellowmen.

High on the list of victims were the Czar's own relatives. His
brother Yuri had died a natural death, but Yuri's widow disappeared in the general holocaust, as did most members of the
late Anastasia's family. Ivan's profound hatred of Kurbsky was
at least partially cooled by the execution of the renegade's wife
and children.

The Czar's own authorized terrorists made it a habit to slay not only the suspect himself, but with him the entire family, even the servants. It was safer this way because of the strong blood bonds in Russian society. No potential avengers were left alive.

In one instance, an *oprichniky* band stormed the castle of a boyar and, together with the master, they killed three hundred of his dependents. The mansion was set afire, and so was the village belonging to it. Even the church went up in flames. Women and children were stripped naked and chased into the fields, whereupon the horsemen, bows in hand, used them for target practice.

For nearly a decade, Russia was in the grips of the terror while, at the borders, the war against Poland and her allies dragged on. When the news from the fronts was bad, the persecutions increased. The higher the rank of a nobleman, the more he was suspected of treason. It did not help the boyars that the king of Poland addressed personally signed letters to some, inviting them to desert. The letters invariably wound up in the hands of Ivan's secret informers.

Those who could did indeed escape, but despite all the outrages, no organized resistance, open or underground, arose. Even the subjects who were persecuted did not question the ruler's right to persecute. His wrath was accepted as one accepts a thunderstorm or an earthquake. One does not rebel against the unfathomable acts of fate.

While Kurbsky compared Ivan IV with Herod, the New Testament slayer of infants, the lower classes continued to champion him as their protector. They were used to rough treatment from their own immediate masters, the Russian aristocracy.

Protracted brutality eventually dehumanizes its perpetrators. It is one thing to inflict pain as a punishment for real or imagined wrongdoings; it is quite another to do it as sport and entertainment. This seems to have occurred at times during Ivan's reign.

Some of the royal banquets became scenes of coarse and cruel jokes. A number of boyars were invited to such a feast. Nobody dared reject a royal invitation. Among the guests was a Prince

Feodor, who had aroused Ivan's suspicion. When the faces had become hot from the strong wine, the Czar bade Feodor sit on his throne. He took off his purple cloak and crown and placed the royal symbols on his guest. "You wanted to sit in my place, boyar," he mocked with an ugly grin. "Here, see how it feels." Before the baffled nobleman could respond, Ivan drew a dagger and ran the victim through, to the thunderous applause of his *oprichniky* companions.

Like other courts, the Kremlin had its jesters, often hunchbacks or otherwise misshappen creatures. They were allowed certain liberties to provide humor, but they could never be sure of the consequences. At one banquet, Gvozdev, Ivan's favorite jester, went too far in his heckling. The master lost his temper. He jumped up and poured a large bowl of piping hot soup over the hapless creature. The cries of pain infuriated Ivan still more. Only after he had used his dagger on the tormented jester did reason return. He summoned Dr. Standish, his physician. "Save him," he demanded. "I have played with my servant imprudently."

"So imprudently," replied the doctor, "that neither God nor Your Majesty will ever make him play again in this world."

Ivan's tragic failing lay in his attempt to play two roles which were incompatible. It was his deep conviction that, as God's anointed, he stood high above his fellowmen, not subject to their judgment. But unable to restrain his animal instincts and being, at the same time, highly sensitive, he realized that he was, after all, only a human being, beset with many human faults.

After the acts of sadistic outrage, he plunged into torments of self-abasement. Bloodying his forehead on the stone floor of the chapel, he cried out: "I am a stinking dog, living in drunkenness, adultery, murder and brigandage."

Monks had to record carefully the names of all his victims on parchment scrolls, and he gave money so that prayers would be said for the repose of their souls. One such entry in the chronicle of St. Cyril Monastery reads:

In the year 7091 [1582, according to the Gregorian calendar] the Czar, Gosudar and Grand Duke Ivan Vasilevich of all Russia gave orders to remember and make daily intercession in the church of God at all liturgical offices and requiem masses . . . of Popov with his wife and son and daughters, of the men of Pskov, with their wives and children, in all seven hundred persons, of twenty men belonging to the village of Kolomenskoe, etc.

After the periods of contrition had passed, the carnage continued. Greed was an added motive. The possessions of all suspects were confiscated. When this did not bring in enough revenue, Ivan thought up other odd schemes. A city was ordered to send him a hatful of fleas for the preparation of some quack medicine. When this proved impossible, as he must have known from the beginning it would, the community was fined seven thousand rubles for disobedience.

What the emperor did not add to his own vast treasure was distributed among the *oprichniky*. These loyal henchmen were mostly landless, and so they received parcels of the confiscated boyar estates in a vast program of land redistribution.

Half-mad with distrust, the Czar avoided, as much as possible, any contact with the court bureaucracy. For prolonged stretches of time he withdrew from the capital altogether and stayed in Alexandrov, where the "revolution from above" had begun. He had a huge fortress erected, complete with ramparts, moats and underground casements. There he lived with several hundred *oprichniky* in rough and ready comradery.

The fortress of Alexandrov was half monastery and half the locale of an ongoing stag party. At four in the morning, the Czar, clad in a black cassock, personally rang the bell for matin services. Hours were spent in prayer and in the veneration of icons. But afterwards he visited the underground dungeon and personally supervised the torturing of prisoners. While they writhed in agony, they were constantly asked, "Where hast thou hidden thy wealth?"

In the afternoon, when the main meal was taken in the refectory, Ivan read aloud from the Scriptures. But afterwards, bawdy jugglers and dancing girls finished out the program.

At prayer, in the torture chambers and at the drunken orgies, the Czarevich, also Ivan by name, was constantly at his father's side. The young man was developing into a carbon copy of the Czar, sharing his talents and his tastes.

Did the older Ivan really want to live like a monk, but was too weak to carry through? Or was the spectacle of Alexandrov meant as a blasphemous mockery of true monasticism from the beginning? Nobody can say with certainty, but it should be pointed out that in several real monasteries conditions were not too different. Wealth and power had corrupted some men of the cloth as they often corrupt men of all stations.

From his dissipations Ivan always returned to his prayers. But he carefully distinguished between personal piety and political goals. The Orthodox faith, yes, but domination by the church, no. No successor to Father Sylvester was allowed near the throne. Priests and monks had better stick to their chanting, or else they might share the lot of the recalcitrant boyars.

The venerable Macary was dead. Ivan's boyhood mentor and long-time head of the Russian church had been a steadying influence on the volatile student. It was time for the bishops and the archimandrites to assemble for the election of a new Metropolitan. Thus it had been from olden times; thus it was to remain. But now a powerful czar wanted to make sure that a person to his liking was elected, and he used his power without hesitation.

Subservience to the throne became a mark of the Russian church, and to this day the state is in control of the religious establishment. The successors to Macary preached unconditional submission to the ruler's will. But not all of them were content to give their blessing to every act of the Czar. Such a heroic exception was the Metropolitan Philip.

Called from a distant monastery where he had been the abbot, Philip, unwillingly and only under royal pressure, accepted the high position. It was customary that, before Sunday services, the Metropolitan would await the Czar at the cathedral entrance to bless him. The ruler approached, but Philip ignored him.

"Don't you see who is standing before you, priest?" shouted the leader of the *oprichniky* guard. "Bless him. He is waiting."

But instead of the blessing, the Metropolitan administered a scathing reproach of the monarch's conduct.

"High as you are on the throne," he said, "there is yet another, our Judge and yours. How, think you, you will stand at His tribunal in the deafening chorus of the cries of the tormented, in the welter of the blood of the innocent?"

"Be silent." Ivan was trembling with rage. "You are one of the rebels. From now on I shall act the way you have described me."

The cleric remained calm. "I am a stranger and a pilgrim on earth, and I am ready to suffer for the truth. Where would my faith be if I kept silent?"

The Czar stormed away. When Philip stepped to the high altar to begin the service, a band of *oprichniky* rushed him. "You have lost your right to this place of honor," they screamed, tearing off his vestments and dragging him away in chains.

The people of Moscow had venerated the Metropolitan, Philip, for his sincere piety. When they heard of his fall from imperial grace, they streamed in large numbers to the prison building where he was held in a dungeon. For long hours they stood there calling for his blessing and praying for his safety.

The prayers were not heeded, at least not as far as the cleric's fate in this world was concerned. He had a visitor, the *oprichnik*

Malyuta Skuratov, the new confidant of the Czar and also his foremost executioner. Skuratov knew that his master was at a loss for what to do about the ungovernable churchman. He took it upon himself to relieve the Czar of having to make any distasteful decision. Skuratov lingered in Philip's cell only a short while. When he left, the Metropolitan lay strangled on the stone floor. Outside the prison, the people heard the news. They fell on their knees and wept. From that day on the Russian Orthodox Church had a new saint.

Ivan was not exactly proud of the reputation his shock troops had acquired, or he would not have tried to hide their existence from foreign eyes and ears. When Russian ambassadors in various countries were asked about the rumors that had seeped abroad, the stock answer was: "*Oprichniky?* Never heard of them. Such stories are the fabrications of Russia's enemies."

But the horsemen kept on riding across the country, sweeping away with their brooms anything that stood in the way of the Czar's power and their own.

11

DEATH *of a* CITY

Unusual activity pervaded the "monastery" of Alexandrov. Hammers were clanging in the smithies. The men sharpened their weapons, and provisions were distributed among the *oprichniky* detachments. The daily meal, usually several hours in length, was cut short.

"Tomorrow we ride," was the order. Nothing was said about the destination. The fortress was asleep at an early hour, except for the sentries at the gates.

At daybreak the drawbridge clanged down. The Czar himself rode at the head of his horsemen. They took the road to the northwest as if to meet a foreign invader, but the mood was relaxed. It was a leisurely trip, with singing, with noisy encampments along the way, with side trips by individual squadrons to loot villages which lay off the main road. Finally it was announced where the force was headed—the city of Novgorod.

Novgorod, situated on the navigable Volkov River, which empties into Lake Ladoga, was a wealthy city long before Moscow was even a hamlet. The merchants of this way station between northern Europe and the Byzantine Empire traded with Germany and with the Hanseatic cities. The cultural climate was sophisticated and oriented towards the West. Both the gentle

Metropolitan, Macary, and the shrewd priest Sylvester had come from Novgorod.

For centuries it had been an independent city state, ruled by a council of the most successful merchants, whose power extended deep into the surrounding countryside. Even after Ivan III had formally annexed Novgorod to the growing Grand Duchy of Moscow, the inhabitants harbored dreams of independence.

Now Russia was at war with Poland and Sweden. Battles raged nearby, followed by periods of quiet. Stories of Ivan's cruelty and of his designs for completely autocratic rule were passed on wherever Novgorodians gathered to do business or to spend an hour over their strong brew.

Perhaps this was the opportunity to slip out from under Moscow's yoke. Poland would have been happy to help. There was a lot of whispering in back rooms; some highly secretive coming and going was observed by people who made it their business to notice such things.

Ivan's spies were on the alert. Novgorod's proud merchant elite had long been a source of irritation to him. For once his eternal suspicion was supported by some shreds of evidence. He also knew that whatever he would do to Novgorod would find approval with Moscow merchants, who looked with unconcealed envy at their northwestern rivals.

He needed a triumph badly. Things were not going well on the battle fronts. His armies were in retreat towards their own borders, with King Stephen in hot pursuit. Fears were ripe among the peasantry and townsfolk in the exposed regions. Something had to be done to boost the general morale.

Conveniently a servant escaped from a wealthy Novgorod home and turned up at Alexandrov with a bit of interesting news: a plot to hand over the city to the Poles. King Stephen had corresponded with Archbishop Pimen and other city leaders. Some of the letters were hidden behind an icon of the Virgin Mary in the Novgorod cathedral. A troop of *oprichniky*, immediately dispatched, found what they were looking for.

Was the evidence genuine, or was it a plant? Nobody was in a position to ask such a question or to investigate the circumstances. In any case, the Czar had his excuse for proceeding against Novgorod and for teaching all real and potential traitors a lesson they would remember.

A regiment of regulars was rushed ahead with orders; "Surround the city. Form a ring so tight that not a soul can get either in or out."

At last Ivan's party, which included his son, arrived at the gates. No resistance was offered; none had been expected. At the high bridge across the Volkov River, the archbishop, surrounded by priests and acolytes, met the sovereign and offered him bread and salt. But when the holy man raised his golden cross to bless Ivan, the Czar rudely slapped it down. "Villain, you are devising plots with traitors. Although you call yourself the shepherd, you are only a wolf, a thief, a murderer."

The prelate backed away in understandable fright, but he was told: "Proceed at once to the cathedral and conduct the service, all of it. Don't dare to leave out a single word."

No chance spectator who watched the stately procession entering the wide-open portals of the candlelit sanctuary would have suspected that the cat was playing with the mouse, relishing its panic before devouring it.

After the last amen had been chanted, the Czar turned to the archbishop. "We have decided to accept your hospitality. Conduct us to your quarters for dinner."

The prelate was startled. Had the witnessing of the divine liturgy changed the heart of the illustrious guest? Or was it part of a devilish design? There was nothing he could do but to accept the role of a gracious host. Bread was broken, and an opulent meal was laid before the cleric and his guests.

While the servants shuttled from the kitchen to the great hall, guests and hosts chatted amiably. The bishop's palace was located inside the Novgorod Kremlin. From its windows the diners could see the cathedral of St. Sophia, with domes of blue, green and gold, with bells hanging in the open belfries and the Orthodox cross high above. Beyond the Kremlin walls stretched the city and the surrounding fields and marshes.

Without warning Ivan rose and gave out a loud yell. The scene changed immediately. Heavily armed *oprichniky* who had kept out of sight stormed into the hall. Some threw themselves at the archbishop while others stormed through palace and cathedral, manhandling priests and carrying off precious vessels and even the crosses and the offerings of the day's worshipers.

The first stage of the master plan was being carried out with exact timing. Ever since the city had been sealed off several days before, the inhabitants had lived in dread. Now armed men rushed through the deserted streets. Guards were placed at the doors of all houses where the leading merchants lived. Church doors were locked so that nobody would be able to seek sanctuary there. Then all monasteries—and there were quite a few—were entered and thoroughly ransacked. This is how the *oprichniky* received their wages. The condemned had to pay their own executioners.

The suspense continued until the next day, when the Czar, with the Czarevich by his side, ascended a wooden platform in the city center. He ordered the prominent citizens brought before him. While their houses were looted, the men were tortured with all sorts of ingenious instruments which the visitors, in their foresight, had brought along. The heir to the throne looked on, unperturbed by the shrieks of the tormented. He was receiving his on-the-spot training in the fine points of statecraft.

Those who survived the tortures were tied to sleds together with their wives and children. The sleds were pushed over a steep embankment into the murky waters of the Volkov. On the bridge stood guardsmen. With long hooks, they pushed bobbing heads under water. A few escaped the men on the bridge. But this possibility had also been taken care of in the meticulous planning. Sharpshooters were stationed farther down-river, and their arrows finished off whoever had survived as far as that point.

Only nightfall brought an end to the carnage, but it was renewed on the next day and on the one after that, every time with fresh batches of human victims. "So great was the disaster," reports an old monastery chronicle, "so terrible was God's wrath at our sins that a thousand persons a day and at times even fifteen hundred were cast into the water."

The figures are probably exaggerated, but it would be hard to exaggerate the feelings of the survivors of one day—wondering whether their turn would come on the following morning.

The river ran red with the blood of Novgorod's citizens. A sickening stench spread across the flatland. It seemed to hang in the crowns of trees, over the grass of the pastures, in clothing and footwear, and it penetrated every building.

The fifth week of the slaughter had arrived, and crushing weariness gripped even the slaughterers. The senses were dull, the arms tired from the whipping and from carrying loot and the feet from stumbling over mounds of corpses. The Czar called a halt and ordered all survivors brought before him. A miserable lot of half-crazed men and women crept from cellars and attics, from stables and storerooms into the presence of their sovereign. They had ceased to care what new fiendish way of torture or execution was awaiting them. Fear had lost its meaning for these benumbed minds.

Hardly a flicker of relief came into their eyes as they heard Ivan proclaim: "Live in peace. No harm will befall you. May all the blood that has been shed fall upon the traitors. As for you, lament no more over all this, but live thankfully in this city."

Unable to utter a word of thanks, they slunk off to their looted homes, over which still hovered the smell of death.

Only Pimen, the archbishop, and the city councillors remained in chains and were sent off to Moscow to await their fate.

Novgorod was dead even though hundreds of dazed inhabitants still lingered in its violated houses. Never again would the city conspire to break the hold of the Rurik reign. Never again would its wealth rival that of the capital. On the banks of the Moskva River, the news of Novgorod's death by collective punishment was received with considerable satisfaction.

One lesson was over, but there were others which needed to be taught. The kettledrums sounded, and the ranks of the *oprichniky* formed once more. With Czar and Czarevich in the lead, they set off for their next assignment.

Not far away lay the city of Pskov, smaller and less important than Novgorod, but similar in character and outlook. It too had been hermetically sealed by an army contingent. The citizens of Pskov knew what had happened to their neighbors. They did not contemplate resistance. The Russian mind was atuned to accept fate as unavoidable. Instead they assembled in their churches to prepare themselves spiritually for the end. The incessant tolling of the church bells could be heard beyond the city walls among the tents of the camping *oprichniky*.

Ivan too heard the tolling bells, and the sound disturbed him. These were the sounds of the religion which he so fervently professed when he was not busy violating its moral principles.

He heard of a hermit, staying nearby, who was rumored to possess mystical powers. His curiosity aroused, Ivan visited the holy man in his cell. The ascetic offered him a slab of raw meat with blood still dripping from it. The Czar shrank back. "Meat? How dare you offer it? Don't you know it is Lent?"

"Why should you care about Lent" was the answer—"you who are getting ready to devour human flesh?"

In deep thought Ivan returned to his tent. He meditated through most of the night, endlessly reciting his prayers. In the morning he ordered his adjutant: "Give the signal to march. We are returning to Moscow."

Pskov was spared.

The Polish war dragged on at a sluggish pace. Few laurels were earned by the Russian forces, yet Ivan returned to his capital as if celebrating a grandiose victory over the national enemy. He rode up to the Kremlin in a style reminiscent of the triumphal entries held by ancient Roman war heroes. The Muscovites played their part by greeting him with thunderous ovations; yet he had vanquished no enemy, only a defenseless city in his own land.

In the dungeons below the palace the leaders of Novgorod and assorted boyars were still waiting—about three hundred all told. The announcement went out that in the morning a public execution would be held on Red Square.

All through the night, workmen hammered and sawed to erect the scaffolds. Greased poles for impaling and damp brush for slow fires were put in readiness. The human mind had always shown considerable inventiveness in devising intricate tools of torture and death.

Usually large crowds would fill the square to partake of such entertainment, to which no admission was charged. But this time, when the Czar and Czarevich, surrounded by their favorites, issued forth from the Kremlin, the square was nearly empty.

Ivan was surprised. Muscovites had finally grown tired of witnessing the endless bloodletting. There was also fear in their hearts. After what had happened in Novgorod, who could be sure that their unpredictable sovereign would not think up some new trick to harm even the citizenry of his own city?

Ivan rode through the empty streets. "There is nothing to be afraid of," he personally assured the people who huddled in the doorways. "No harm will overtake you." Only then did the plaza begin to fill. The show could begin.

With a mass of less than enthusiastic spectators before him, the Czar became doubtful about the wisdom of the whole proceedings. His mood turned benign. The prisoners were brought out, many half-dead from the tortures. Of the three hundred, only about a hundred were turned over to the henchman. The others received last-minute reprieves, among them Archbishop Pimen, who was exiled to a distant monastery.

The vast square rang with the shouts: "God bless the Czar."

So ended the tale of the death of a proud city. The details were carefully written down in the chronicle of the Pskov Monastery, which places the total number of victims at 60,000. Some historians feel that two thousand would be a more credible figure. But whether one takes the larger or the smaller figure, the rape of Novgorod remains the most appalling chapter in the history of Ivan the Terrible's misdeeds. It could very well have served as a model for a number of atrocities committed in the present century. During the Second World War, the Nazi authorities repeatedly wiped out entire villages as reprisal for the assassination of a single German. The whole idea of the collective punishment of innocent people for the real or alleged crimes of individuals runs contrary to the most elemental concepts of justice.

But in sixteenth-century Russia nobody raised the question of justice. The Czar had made his point. Death and destruction were the lot of those who would even whisper of defection or opposition. But what he did to Novgorod and what his *oprichniky* horsemen did to many thousands, some guilty and many innocent, brought suffering to all of Russia at a time when battles raged on the frontiers and hostile armies hacked at each other in wild savagery.

Beset by the threat of foreign invasion and at the same time fearing persecution by fellow Russians, the people became confused and listless. Why work and plan for the future when it looked so uncertain? The constant strife once again depleted the resources of the potentially rich and fertile country. Fields remained untilled. Whole villages were deserted as peasants tried to escape the exorbitant war taxes.

In 1570 one of the worst famines swept the Eastern European plains. The poor were reduced to eating straw and tree bark. Epidemics further reduced the population. Instances of cannibalism were reported, and famished dogs could be seen chewing unburied human corpses. Superstition attributed the disaster to an elephant which the Shah of Persia had sent to Ivan as a gift along with its keeper. Beast and keeper were killed, but the plague continued.

This was the moment that the Tatars chose to revive their old ambitions. Beaten in many campaigns and now nominally a subject of the Czar, the Crimean khan could still mobilize thousands of swift raiders. With hunger stalking Russian towns, with the armies busy against the Poles, he grasped his chance.

In secret collaboration with Moscow's enemies, 200,000 horsemen swept up to the gates of Moscow, encountering almost no resistance. Khan Devlet Herei challenged the Czar to a personal combat, but swordplay was not one of Ivan's favorite sports. In fact, he was not even in the capital, having fled to the safety of Vologda, a country town.

Even in Vologda Ivan had to endure further humiliation. The Khan sent an envoy to demand submission and payment of a hefty tribute. When Ivan sat quietly among his clerks pondering his answer, the Tatar burst out, "My master, the Lord of all Lords, sends you a gift, Grand Duke, to console yourself in your defeat. Here is a knife with which to cut your throat." Both gift and demand were refused.

In Moscow the raiders set fire to the houses in the outskirts, and a brisk wind spread the flames into the city. Once more Moscow was a heap of smoldering ruins, a giant graveyard. So complete was the destruction that the Tatars did not even stay to loot. Swiftly as they had come, they vanished into the southern steppe.

"It was the hand of God punishing me for my sins," exclaimed the Czar. Why were so many punished who did not commit them? Such a question he did not ask.

When he returned to the capital, the Moskva River was still choked with the bodies of those who had tried to escape the fire. Many were weighted down with the possessions they had tried to carry with them. For months afterwards, survivors fished in the polluted water for rings and for bags of gold and silver.

From his palace the Czar looked out over the landscape of death. Here he was in the year 1571, forty-one years old. After having labored for over three decades to build a strong nation, he now sat amidst the ruins of his capital, not knowing when the Tatars would return to finish off what remained.

The Tatars did indeed return a year later, but this time a Russian army was ready for them at the Oka River behind square barricades of wagons. Confronted with organized resistance, the horsemen lost all stomach for fight. They retreated in haste, leaving large numbers of prisoners, servants and camp followers to the pursuers.

Russia had come close to ruin. Was it to collapse so soon after it had begun to rise? Tragic setbacks had hit the nation before, and severe strokes of misfortune were to hit it again. But Russians, individually and collectively, have shown incredible recuperative power. Hardships are borne with grim fatalism, and then one picks up the pieces and begins anew.

The Czar, too, possessed this built-in resilience. Once he got over his period of sulking and self-pity, he plunged into new stratagems to keep Russia alive despite all obstacles.

The dreams of conquest had to be pushed into the back of his mind for the time being. More pressing was the need for food, the basic necessity. The black earth of Russia is among the richest in the world. Its grains and vegetables could feed many nations if only men were available to plant and harvest them. Russia was then and was to remain primarily an agricultural country, a nation of peasants who drew their strength from the nutritious soil.

The farmland was crying out for the plow and the harrow, guided by human hands. But human hands were scarce and were becoming scarcer. Peasant boys were fighting the Poles. Others flocked to the cities in quest of excitement. Many more were moving out into the endless forest regions as pioneers to hack out, amidst the tall trees, a new and freer existence.

Something had to be done. Ivan began to set in motion, haltingly at first, a development that was to put its stamp on Russian society almost until our own time. The plowman became tied to the soil he worked.

Traditionally the Russian peasant had been an independent sort of fellow. His life was rough, but he fought on his own terms, clearing his patch where he found a knoll of high land or a loamy stretch by the river. When new frontiers beckoned, he packed up and moved. Even as a crop sharing tenant, he was free to seek another landlord provided his debts were paid to the previous one. Noble landowners often competed for experienced farmers. With various promises of better working and living conditions they tried to lure them away to their own estates.

This had to be stopped. A series of decrees issued forth from the Kremlin during the 1570s that gradually restricted the freedom of the peasantry. At first, families were allowed to move only on certain days of the year. The number of these days decreased until, by 1581, the peasant found himself nailed to a piece of ground for life. The free yeoman had become a *kholop* (serf). He belonged to the land as the trees and the grass belonged to it, and he was bought, sold, inherited and willed with the land. Whoever owned the land owned the peasant. The landlord became the peasant's judge, prosecutor, taskmaster, rent collector and executioner.

This was the Russian peasant under the Czars—barefoot, clad in summer in a loose sacklike gown of coarse material, protected from the winter cold by a sheepskin, working from dawn to dusk.

In the world beyond the eastern plains, serfdom had been a fixture of social and economic life ever since the dying days of the Roman Empire. But with the waning of the Middle Ages it began to disappear in the rest of Europe, having outlived its usefulness. Then it gained a firm foothold in the Rurik empire, introduced to the estates of the boyars and the serving gentry at the behest of their autocratic ruler. It became the mode of the land so that Russians could have their wheat and barley, their flax and hemp, and it was not legally abolished until the same year that the United States of America emancipated its slaves.

The serf was at the mercy of his landlord, just as all Russians were to obey unquestioningly their Little Father. Fugitive serfs were hunted down and punished with all the barbaric severity typical of the time. But when a landlord was particularly cruel or when the stories of the endless free forest sounded too enticing, many still stole away in the dead of night, on crude river rafts or on foot. Serfdom did not crush the pioneering spirit; if anything, it hardened it.

Did the poor people curse the Czar for the loss of their freedom? No. They hated their overlords passionately, but they continued to venerate the monarch. The more savage the ferocity with which he fought his own aristocracy, the more they felt that he was on their side—a champion of the little people.

12
RETREAT

Hunger and plague, Poles and Tatars had united to torment the Russian empire, so young and still beset by growing pains. The major Tatar bands were finally pacified, and in a few more generations the warriors on horseback would be transformed into peaceful shepherds and traders. But the Czar was deeply worried. His realm had come perilously close to being wiped out. The hours of silent brooding lengthened, filled with forebodings of doom.

Once again his mistrust had been justified. The *oprichniky* had failed him. Created to make a state out of chaos, this instrument of authoritarianism broke down pitifully at the crucial moment when the enemy threatened from outside. It had been good enough for pillaging boyars' castles and chasing defenseless women, but not for warding off the Tatar onslaught. The devil's black horsemen, so dreaded by their countrymen, simply faded away when the khan's raiders approached, when Moscow was destroyed and its women and ablebodied men were carried off into slavery.

The Tatars, on their return visit were finally beaten back, but it was not the Czar's favorites with their brooms and dog's heads who put them to flight, but old-line boyar generals leading well-trained *streltsi* and foreign mercenaries.

After what must have been a violent inner struggle, Ivan admitted that it had all been a giant mistake. The whole system of the *oprichnina* was abolished. From then on the hunters became the hunted. Former favorites of the throne were labeled traitors, and many tasted their own medicine—the various refined and prolonged methods of torture and execution.

The aristocracy of the *zemshchina* had emerged as the only group of men capable of giving military and executive leadership. With all their shortcomings, they remained the main reservoir for drawing talent for public service. Once more they were called upon to man the courts of justice and all the important governmental posts.

But they were not the proud boyar class of old. The blood-letting during the days of the *oprichniky* had shattered their pride. Now they knew who was their boss. They still held power, but only as it was delegated to them from the throne. They rendered advice only when asked, and they had to give a reckoning of their actions.

From then on, the Czar treated the nobility as individuals and not as a class, rewarding some and punishing others, according to his judgment. The boyars had ceased to be a decision-making body.

The first Russian experiment in totalitarian rule based on terror and intimidation was over. Others were to follow later.

All through the years of inner convulsion, the Poles and Swedes kept up the pressure on the frontiers, vigorously cheered on by Russian nobles in exile. Stephen Batory, informed of his enemy's internal troubles, decided that the moment had come for a decisive stroke. The dynamic Polish king was convinced that the two Slavic nations were not meant to live peacefully side by side as equals. Sooner or later one would attempt to dominate the other. As he saw the situation, Poland now had her chance to do the dominating. If he could knock out Moscow with a decisive stroke, his would be an empire stretching from the German lands to the Ural Mountains. It was a grandiose vision, worth a valiant try.

Feverish preparations were made in armories and on parade grounds, while Catholic priests tried to stir up a new crusading fervor. Freshly outfitted Polish armies, augmented by hirelings from many nations, poured into the regions claimed by Ivan. Initial successes were extremely encouraging.

The king was a stern taskmaster. His orders were to refrain from looting, to respect the civilian population. But even though he took the field in person and ceaselessly inspected the troops, he could not prevent outrages similar to the ones Russian troops had perpetrated on Livonian cities. The old rule prevailed that the soldier's price for risking his life was to pillage the houses of the conquered and to make sport with their women.

But when his armies crossed into Russia proper, it soon became evident that he had miscalculated. There was no wholesale defection as he had hoped. Too deeply ingrained in the Russian mind was the obedience to authority. With stubbornness and bravery, peasants, burghers and nobles rallied to defend their own soil. This was what they could do best, as many a war was to prove in the future. The city of Pskov was a key bastion in the Russian defense system. Stephen Batory laid siege, but instead of a quick conquest he encountered heroic resistance. Finally, after his troops wearied of the protracted costly assaults, the siege was lifted. It was a Russian triumph of sorts, and it raised the troubled spirit of the Czar.

But by now Ivan realized that this was a war which could not be won. The country was exhausted. To the south the Turks were patiently waiting for Russia to weaken herself to the point of impotence, and there still lurked some independent Tatar khans deep in the southern steppes who harbored similar hopes. The country needed peace, even at the cost of a stalemate.

Again he resorted, to the wily game of diplomacy. While soldiers slaughtered each other on the battlefields, Russian emissaries, traveling openly and in secret, visited the Polish court to bargain. Stephen was not completely unreceptive, for he had his own troubles. The treasury was exhausted, and the proud Polish nobility resented the king's popularity. He was, after all, a foreigner, and therefore not overly concerned with preserving their old privileges.

Still, he was asking a steep price. The Czar was to give up not only all he had previously conquered, but also vast stretches of Lithuanian lands which his father and grandfather had annexed. This price the Czar was unwilling to pay.

He looked for outside mediators, and he decided to approach a most unlikely candidate for this task.

Decked out with Moscow's customary pomp, and carrying chests filled with costly gifts, a large embassy set out on a long journey. They crossed the Alps into the balmy valleys of northern Italy and continued southward until they sighted the massive dome of St. Peter's Basilica in Rome. The foremost defender of the Eastern Orthodox faith laid his case before Pope Gregory XIII, spiritual head of Catholicism, which Ivan had often denounced as a devilish form of heresy.

Was this the senseless splashing around of a man about to drown? Not at all. Ivan had not lost his shrewd mind. He knew very well that the Pope would be interested, and indeed he was.

If the fur-cloaked Russians had been a strange sight in the streets of Rome, the appearance of a papal delegation in Moscow some months later was at least as sensational. Clean-shaven clerics in black and crimson habits were driven to the Kremlin in gilded carriages surrounded by their Swiss escorts, who wore striped corselets and shining brass helmets and shouldered long halberds.

The Pope's chief negotiator was the Jesuit Antonio Possevino. Ushered into Ivan's presence, he found himself in a place which resembled a church more than a throne room. Frescoes of saints adorned all four walls. From above the massive golden throne, a stern Christ with a wide golden halo looked straight at the visitor.

After transmitting the Holy Father's blessing and handing over some exquisite presents, the Jesuit came straight to the point. Yes, the Holy See would be glad to mediate a cease-fire. Though the Orthodox Church persisted in grievous doctrinal errors, it was, nevertheless, a Christian church. Now was the time for all Christians to draw together against the common enemy—the Turkish infidels, who acknowledged neither the divinity of Christ nor His virgin birth.

Ivan smiled, but kept his thoughts to himself. He realized what the Pope was up to. What a triumph it would be for him to have both eastern and western Christians fight together under his leadership against the disciples of Muhammad. Possevino, not very adept at concealing his thoughts, made it quite obvious that a return to the Catholic fold would be the expected compensation for the service of mediation.

Being by far the better diplomat, Ivan easily strung the papal representative along. He was, as always, most willing to converse with him about theology. Mostly he remained calm; only once did his temper get the better of him, and he shouted: "Your Roman Pope is not a shepherd at all, he is a wolf."

Yet the Jesuit never gave up hope for the Russian's conversion. Dutifully he shuttled between Moscow and Cracow, month after month, trying to the best of his limited ability to break the deadlock.

In the meantime, Ivan did not remain idle. He explored other avenues to win points in the international power game. He had collected many enemies, but he had kept one friend—England. The British commercial agents had spread a network of trading outlets all over the empire. Russia became the economic link between London and the fabulous markets of the Far East.

As guests of the Czar, the Britishers had to honor his whims and moods. The close supervision, the snooping and interfering were quite annoying, but it was worth the price. The Russian trade became enormously profitable, for the British economy was still locked in a life and death struggle with Spaniards, Portuguese and Dutchmen. While England received much, it gave comparatively little in return.

Ivan renewed his orders to all provincial governors to cooperate with the Englishmen and to respect their customs. Personally he continued to enjoy their company, and he listened eagerly to their reports about the rich cultural life in London, now in its most glorious period. Shakespeare was growing to manhood. The city on the Thames was alive with philosophical and theological disputations, new scientific experiments and the ambitious schemes of politicians.

Ivan wanted more from England than just friendly trade relations. In message after message he exhorted the young queen to conclude a strong military alliance with him. Elizabeth's answers were polite, but noncommital. She was all for a casual friendship with Russia. The two countries had no conflicting interests; but more binding pacts, involving troops and naval craft, were quite another matter. The Queen had no intention of fighting somebody else's wars. She wanted manpower and weaponry conserved for Britain's far-reaching designs overseas. There, across the oceans, a world-girdling empire was waiting to be conquered.

The Queen's answer, clothed in the usual diplomatic jargon of pious generalities, was a distinct "no."

The correspondence between the two sovereigns sheds some light on Ivan's deep-seated feeling of insecurity. He proposed a mutual understanding that, if one would be forced to leave his country, the other would give him asylum. Elizabeth could not see herself in the role of a political refugee, but she promised Ivan, through her ambassador in Moscow, that should the need arise, he would be "friendly received into our dominions, and shall find assured friendship in us. Besides, we shall appoint you, the Emperor and Grand Duke, a place in our kingdom fit upon your own charges, as long as you shall like to remain with us."

Even more astounding was another proposition. What about a marriage between Rurik Czar and Tudor monarch? The queen was still single; the Czar was not, but there were nunneries aplenty in his land. Ivan commissioned his friends of the Russian Company to sound out Elizabeth on their next trip back to London. As he saw it, one British queen had married the Spanish ruler, so why couldn't another do the same with the Russian, thereby uniting the largest mass of land with the most formidable realm stretching over the seven seas?

It could be an interesting thought game to speculate what the course of history would have been like if this unlikely couple really had stepped to the altar.

But Elizabeth was not in a marrying mood, not then or ever after. Ivan, little used to having his wishes denied by a mere woman, tried a different approach. If he could not have the Queen, how about another English lady of high rank? The idea of obtaining a wife from the island kingdom had become an obsession.

From the British residents in Moscow he heard of Lady Marie Hastings, a niece of the Queen who was, as luck would have it, available. Her age—in her thirties—was just about right for the fifty-two-year-old suitor.

An envoy, Count Pissemsky, was hastily dispatched to London to look her over. "Report to me," he was instructed, "about her complexion, her height, if she is not too thin for my taste and if she would be willing to embrace my faith."

Obviously Ivan was convinced that any woman anywhere would jump at such a chance, but again he was in for a painful disappointment. When Pissemsky turned to the queen for help, she brushed him off with all sorts of excuses: the lady was ill; the lady had suffered from smallpox and was too ashamed to show her blemished face.

Elizabeth sympathized with her niece's reluctance to be installed in the Kremlin *terem*. Always tactful, she wrote to Ivan: "I do not find her beautiful, and I cannot imagine that she would be found so by such a connoisseur of beauty as my brother Ivan." Apparently news of the Czar's keen interest in the fairer sex had traveled all the way to the banks of the Thames.

This time Ivan was really furious, not so much at Lady Hastings as at her queen. If Elizabeth had really ordered this woman to marry the Czar or anybody else, how could she have refused? In Russia this would have been unthinkable. What kind of a ruler was she anyhow that she had so little power over her subjects? In deep resentment he wrote:

We thought that you were ruler in your own land, seeking your own honor. But now we see you are ruled by other men, and what men—like merchants, like peasants. They do not seek the honor of our two Majesties, while you act like a stupid wench and nothing else.

For him a monarch whose will was not supreme just was not a monarch.

But here he had to acknowledge a limit to his power. He could sputter and storm all he wanted; Lady Hastings remained safe and sound in her home country. For a time, the British residents in Russia had to bear the brunt of Ivan's ruffled pride. He withdrew some privileges from the Russian Company and refused to receive its representatives. It took a long time before his genuine liking for the British visitors overcame his resentment.

All this courting, however unsuccessful, indicated how little he cared for his own wife, Maria. More than a decade after the death of the beloved Anastasia, he still spoke and wrote of her as if she had departed only the day before. So it was not surprising that he showed no sorrow at Maria's death in 1569. Nor did his subjects. She was put to rest with all the proper ceremonies, but it was all done in unseemly haste. As usual, rumors persisted that the hapless spouse had been poisoned at the Czar's own instigation. Under the circumstances, it was not at all unlikely.

In his repeated periods of remorse and self-pity, during which he compared his suffering with the trials of Job, Ivan frequently expressed the desire to give up the throne and retire to live the life of a monk.

In 1575, he once again announced his abdication. This time he did not just ride off as he had done before; he appointed his own successor. To the consternation of the whole court, it turned out to be Simeon, a Tatar prince who, like other Tatars, had accepted Russian domination.

Simeon was duly installed on the throne. Ivan bowed before him and vowed to obey his every command. Outwardly at least, he kept the vow. Whenever he came to call, he humbly announced: "Ivan Vasilievich, Prince of Moscow, has come to do homage to Your Majesty."

Was this another of his cruel jokes? No; his dagger remained sheathed, and Simeon, a man of limited intelligence, kept crown and purple mantle for two full years.

Nobody got hurt, yet it turned out to be a comedy of sorts after all. No doubt existed in anybody's mind that Ivan was in command, though all edicts were proclaimed in the name of Czar Simeon.

Why the comedy? The Czar had not lost his old penchant for play-acting. Had fate made him an Englishman, he might have joined Shakespeare on the stage. But there was more to it than role-playing. As he humbled himself before Simeon, he demonstrated by example to all Russians how they were expected to humble themselves before the throne no matter who occupied the seat of authority.

His temporary retirement further turned out to be a trick to straighten out the state finances. It amounted to a disguised declaration of bankruptcy. The pseudo-czar immediately canceled all royal debts. Then he confiscated a lot of church and monastery property. Unfavorable criticism would fall on his head, not on that of Ivan, for whom he acted as whipping boy. When confronted with all sorts of adversities, the real Czar in this manner succeeded in employing the old oriental technique of "saving face."

The fact that Simeon was a Tatar also symbolized the attempt at unifying the various ethnic groups now under the Rurik crown.

Taking back the crown proved to be as smooth an operation as giving it away. Simeon was pensioned off, and without a murmur of protest he retired to a comfortable country estate. During his remaining years, he signed all correspondence with the crown as "Your most obedient slave."

Ivan remained the Czar, and he never became a monk. He had played with monasticism in the days of the *oprichniky,* but it was a mockery of true monasticism, which, among other things, required constant chastity. This was not for the man who displayed such a voracious appetite for women throughout his life. Love was dead, but sex remained, both of the marital and the extramarital variety.

For the third time he decided to marry. Again the call went out through the land, and the most desirable virgins assembled in the capital. Again the beauty contest was held; only this time there were two winners instead of one. Ivan Ivanovich, the Czarevich, was now of marriageable age. It seemed practical to kill two birds with one stone. Together father and son marched down the row of blushing maidens who had survived the initial screening. Two handkerchiefs were thrown into two laps; two weddings were held, a few days apart.

The Czar lost his third wife after only two weeks. In their screening, the not very skillful physicians had apparently overlooked a serious ailment from which the candidate suffered. This should have been the end of Ivan's marital ventures, for the Eastern Orthodox Church allows a man only three marriages. But he was not just a man; he was the Czar. Under heavy pressure, the church authorities bent the law especially for him. The servile Metropolitan found a loophole by asserting that the third marriage had not been consummated, so it did not count as a marriage at all.

Wife number four graced the royal court for three years before she was packed off to a nunnery. Her entire family was murdered so that there would be no complaints from disgruntled relatives.

Altogether Ivan accumulated seven consorts during his lifetime. With two of them—numbers five and six, to be exact—he lived without the benefit of a religious ceremony. Little is known about these ladies, since they were kept isolated in the *terem,* where few Russian males and almost no foreigners ever saw them. Historians and biographers may argue whether they should be referred to as wives or as mistresses and whether therefore the number of spouses should be set at five or seven.

Czarevich Ivan turned out to be much like his father. He married three times and sent two of his wives off to nunneries.

While a succession of female favorites entered and left the royal *terem,* the war and, simultaneously, the attempts to make peace, dragged on. Both sides, Russians and Poles, were exhausted, and both were beset with pressing internal difficulties. At long last, a ten-year truce was signed. Nobody could claim victory. The Russian forces withdrew from the Baltic coast, except for the extreme tip of the Gulf of Finland. Another half century was to go by until Peter the Great was finally to wrench the "window to the Baltic" wide open.

Father Possevino packed his cassocks and his scrolls for the return trip to Rome. Half his mission was accomplished: the muskets and arquebuses were silent. But the other half was a failure. The Russian Church did not reenter the fold. The Czar even forbade the erection of a Catholic house of worship anywhere within his realm.

Seen from the vantage point of Russian power politics, the long, bloody struggle was not fought completely in vain. A claim had been established. A new big power was knocking at the door of Europe demanding entrance. The defense of their soil had united the Russian people behind their Czar. Despite his cruelty, he remained the pivot of unity, praised from border to border in story and song.

13
EASTWARD HO

"That Yermak, the Cossack hetman, is making trouble again," reported the *dyak*.

The Czar had just finished his long prayers. His mind was still on things spiritual, and he was angry at being interrupted by disagreeable affairs of state.

"What is that chief of brigands up to now? Can't you deal with a band of outlaws without bothering me?"

"This is more than common robbery, Your Majesty. The report just came in that they have attacked a large caravan of Russian traders only a short distance from Astrakhan. They carried off all the merchandise, and they are holding the travelers for ransom."

"This has to be stopped." The Czar stamped his foot, and the wrinkled brow forewarned a stormy outburst. "Send a strong army contingent after them. They must bring back Yermak dead or alive, or I will see that they suffer for it."

The soldiers set out after the Cossack leader, but they never got a glimpse of him. He had vanished.

The Cossacks, made up of peasants who had escaped their landlords, fugitives from Tatar raids and assorted adventurers and smaller border tribes, formed tight communities along the

Don River in southeastern Russia. In the rough democratic
spirit of a warrior brotherhood, they elected their hetman or
leader. There existed no social classes. Every Cossack was at the
same time a farmer and a soldier, ready at all hours to drop
the plow and jump on his trusted horse. Nominally they were
Russian subjects, and when it pleased them they fought the
Czar's wars. But mostly they acted as the moment's advantage
dictated it, attacking Poles today and plundering the caravans
of loyal merchants tomorrow. Famed for their dashing courage
and recklessness, the Cossack warriors spread terror wherever
they appeared.

Cossacks liked to live dangerously. Either they died in the
saddle or they won and then celebrated with riotous gaiety.

When Yermak's spies reported the approach of a strong Russian force, he found it wise to withdraw. His men had often
fought Tatars; in fact, through the veins of some rolled Tatar
blood. Adopting the time-honored tactics of those mounted nomads, the five hundred brothers melted into the trackless steppe.
No choice was left to the pursuers but to return and face the
sovereign's displeasure.

What next? The Cossack thrived best in thinly populated
country, where he could roam freely and attack with lightning
surprise. The land which formerly belonged to the Crimean
khan was beginning to fill up. Villages were springing up at
river crossings populated by serfs who had escaped their masters.
It was time to move on, and all signs pointed to the east.

So they turned their horses in the direction of the densely
wooded Ural Mountains. Daggers and sabers were freshly honed;
the knouts dangled from the saddles. Their lusty songs filled the
grass- and flower-scented air as they rode along, keeping a sharp
lookout for unescorted travelers and isolated settlements to re-
plenish their supplies along the way.

After many days, they entered a wide clearing in the foothills
of the Urals. There were fields of rye and oats. A timber stockade,
twelve feet high, surrounded a cluster of imposing log buildings.

From the chimneys smoke rose and lost itself in the white clouds.

Armed men stood on the watchtowers, motionless, their muskets at the ready. Fire flashed from the muzzle of a cannon, and its thunder rolled over the treetops in a stern warning. But no iron ball emerged; only the powder had been exploded to signal that this settlement was not to be trifled with.

The tall Cossack chief rode forward. When he lifted his fur cap and waved his arm, the long blond hair tumbled in the breeze. "We come as friends," he shouted, "to serve the great lord Stroganov. Our swords are at his command."

The heads of the sentries disappeared. After what must have been a long period of parleying inside the stockade, the heavy gate of Chusavaya slowly creaked open. Trim and proud, the Cossacks rode into the wide courtyard, sabers twirling over their heads. From tiny upper-story windows peered the dark eyes of women excited about the welcome break in the monotony of frontier life.

The horses were tethered and fed. Fires flared in the yard. The men of Chusavaya sat down with the Cossacks to a feast of bear meat, venison and dark bread, washed down with huge quantities of potent *quas*. Ribald jokes caused bellowing laughter. A horseman retrieved his balalaika from the saddlebag, and as he began to pluck the strings, men began to dance. Faster and faster they twirled and jumped as only Cossacks, with their boundless stamina, can.

Meanwhile, in the manor house, the brothers Simeon and Maxim Stroganov sat down to dinner with Yermak and his chief lieutenants. In the hall the walls were covered with damask cloth the color of dark wine. Candles blazed in silver chandeliers. In gold and silver dishes servants brought exquisitely prepared food. Hungarian wine sparkled in golden goblets. Soft music played by strings and woodwinds issued from the balcony. The visitors had entered an island of highly sophisticated civilization in the midst of the endless untamed forest.

Women joined the men at the table. Not forced under the yoke of Moscow tradition, they led a freer life here. Clad in a gown of silk brocade, Olga, the beautiful sister of the Stroganovs, offered Yermak his first goblet of wine. "Drink, noble lord," she said, blushing deeply. "The house of my father is your house."

The bearded giant bowed, and when she offered her cheek for the welcome kiss, his lips lingered on the rosy skin much longer than etiquette required. Admiration and soon more than that was mirrored in Olga's finely chiseled face as she listened to Yermak's tales of wild Cossack exploits.

More wine appeared at the table. The voices grew louder, and the candle flames appeared to become shrouded in a haze. When Koltzo, the hetman's chief aide, made some too personal remarks about Olga's charms, Yermak jumped up fuming. His curved saber was out of its sheath in a split second, and a bright red mark appeared on Koltzo's arm. Only when he saw the blood trickle to the floor did the love-struck Cossack regain his calm. Everybody resumed his seat. The conversation continued as if nothing had happened.

After the table was cleared, the men got around to discussing what was foremost on their minds, though Yermak had a hard time concentrating on matters of commerce and welfare.

They were sitting at the edge of two continents. Though its highest peaks reach only a little over six thousand feet, the Ural range is the traditional dividing line between Europe and Asia. Ivan's conquest of Kazan had also made it the boundary of Russia. Into this uncharted expanse of tundra in the north, forest in the middle and grassland in the south moved the pioneers, clearing the forest, building cabins and laying their traps for silver fox, sable and ermine. Among them were peasants and boyars, those who had to fear justice and those who just wanted to escape tyranny, the tyranny of serfdom or the tyranny of absolutism.

The new settlers continued to recognize the Czar in Moscow

as their lawful and divinely ordained ruler, but they organized their lives pretty much as they pleased. Moscow was far away. The threat of governmental retribution carried little weight here.

The Stroganovs were the uncrowned kings of this hardy pioneer society. Old Anika Stroganov, a man of plucky peasant stock, was the patriarch of the family, and under his stern guidance the sons had built a far-flung trading empire.

As long as the *oprichniky* existed, the Stroganovs had been members of the notorious brotherhood, but their membership was a mere formality. Their regular shipments of furs and gold were welcome contributions to the royal treasury. The Czar gratefully acknowledged these tokens of loyalty. Though he was preoccupied with his political designs in the west, it gradually dawned on him that developments on the eastern frontier might eventually turn out to be of even greater impact on Russia's future.

The Stroganovs were granted generous privileges. Under a government which, as a rule, monopolized and controlled most economic activity, Anika's sons had a surprisingly free hand to mine gold, salt and iron. It soon became evident that the mineral wealth of the tree-covered mountains was inexhaustible. The Stroganovs also developed an extensive trade in fur, spices and costly textiles, brought from inner Asia on the ancient caravan trails.

Like the Hudson's Bay Company in the early days of North American colonization, the brothers actually ruled a sizable empire, with fields and pastures, herds of cattle and a city that contained shops of all kinds, including even a cannon foundry. At their command was a private army of marksmen ready to defend this commercial empire against Tatar bands which still penetrated from across the Urals. Inside their spacious mansion, Simeon and Maxim held court like princes in an atmosphere of luxury and refinement.

Days before Yermak appeared at their gate, the Stroganovs had known about the approach of his band. News travels fast even in the sparsely populated forest. The name of the warrior chief was well known. His exploits had become legend and were told and retold at campsites all over the frontier lands.

At the bedside of Anika, who was now feeble of body but still alert in mind, the family held serious council. Was Yermak to be received with banquets or with bullets? The soldiers of the frontier fort, though few in number, were well trained. Arms were plentiful. Chusavaya could give any comer a good fight.

But the Stroganovs were not thirsting for a fight, not unless it was unavoidable or to their advantage. First and foremost, they were calculating merchants, wise in the ways of the frontier. They too had their network of informers, and they were well aware of what was going on on both sides of the Urals.

East of the mountains, the plains continued in an endless spread all across Asia to the Pacific Ocean. It was the same type of land—more tundra, more forest and more steppe, with supplies of furs, timber, gold and who knew what other treasures, in quantities which surpassed human imagination. Their pioneer blood was restless, their pioneer legs itched to strike out for all this abundance which was beckoning just beyond the horizon.

It was not just a question of expanding the commercial empire; there were pressing problems requiring immediate attention. Just east of the mountain range extended Sibir, the land of the Tatar Khan Kuchum. One of the many splinters that remained from the mammoth empire of Genghis Khan, it eventually gave its name to the whole northern tier of the continent —Siberia.

For a time, Khan Kuchum had recognized Moscow's sovereignty and paid a yearly tribute of a thousand sable furs. But hearing reports of Ivan's troubles, he felt the time had come to turn the tables. Sibir commandos began to feel their way across the Ural passes. Sneak attacks on isolated pioneer stations became frequent. Some bands had penetrated too close to the Stroganov stronghold itself for comfort.

Reports were sent to the Czar together with urgent requests for help. But Ivan's mind was absorbed by troubles closer at hand. Even if substantial help could have been sent, roads were practically nonexistent. The pioneer community was left to its own resources.

The sons informed the ailing father: "The men of Sibir are raiding our herds and destroying the outlying forts. The tribesmen who remain loyal to us are frightened. They run into the deep forest at the first sight of a Tatar arrow."

The old man thought long. Then he spoke slowly. "Yermak wants to fight, so let him have his fight. Let him conquer Sibir for us."

The brothers looked at each other, their eyes shining. "Well spoken, Father. If he succeeds, he will find much to loot. And who has ever heard of a Cossack who disdains loot?"

"He can get more than loot. He will regain the Czar's favor. From a hunted outlaw he will turn into a hero."

"And if he doesn't succeed?"

"Well, neither he nor any of his men will live to tell the tale. Then we will just have to trust in God and in our cannons."

This was why Yermak was greeted at Chusavaya with open arms, why he was wined and dined and why he had occasion to fall in love with the graceful Olga.

The Cossack embraced the Stroganov plan with fervor. In his heart mingled the greed of a robber with the valor of a medieval knight in armor, who thirsted to measure his strength against incredible odds. And in the spirit of chivalry, not generally found among Russian males, he wanted to return to Olga and lay the spoils of victory at her feet.

He called his men together. "Brothers, in a few days we will ride against Sibir. We will burn the Tatar yurts, and we will carry off their women. Our saddlebags will bulge with gold, and our grandchildren will sing the praise of our deeds. Brothers, be ready, be brave."

They responded with thunderous cheers. This was good Cossack talk.

More pleasant days followed with more gracious meals, more music and dancing and more hours spent in the company of Olga. One incident marred this serene period of preparation. A pagan seer was brought into the house, a shaman. According to Tatar belief, he could converse with the spirits and wrest from them the secrets of the future.

Slowly he went through his weird ritual of conjuring up what was hidden to other human minds. Then he proclaimed: "Yermak the Bold, leader of brave men, you will conquer and you will gain glory and wealth. They will sing of your deeds at the campfires. But I see a double-headed eagle which will descend upon you and will tear out your heart. Thus speak the great spirits."

Yermak laughed. Who had ever heard of an eagle with two heads? This savage was mocking him. He drew his blade. This time it did more than scratch the skin. The severed head of the careless soothsayer rolled in the dust.

Through the wide-open gate of the stockade rode the Cossacks, singing their battle songs. Behind them followed eight hundred well-armed Stroganov guards. Yermak, in the lead, had a silken handkerchief knotted around his neck, a good-bye gift from his lady-love, who stood at a window with tears streaking her lovely cheeks. Soon the forest swallowed up the little army.

Their route towards the rising sun was long and tortuous. The Siberian plain is divided by long rivers, all rolling northward towards the Arctic Sea. The invaders made slow progress floating down one river on barges, crossing to the next on land and then rowing upstream in a zigzag progression.

No Tatars could be seen, but with their fine sense of the wilderness and their long experience, the Cossacks knew that they were around, hiding behind trees and clumps of tall grass.

Yermak knew better than to be lured by the enemy to follow

him into the boundless steppe. The Cossacks camped on the riverbanks, with sentries watching over the sleepers. Even so, there were sudden attacks in the dead of night.

A number of small skirmishes took place. The invaders emerged victorious, although they were heavily outnumbered. Still, Cossack graves had to be dug by the rivers, and seriously wounded men had to be left behind. With every engagement, the size of the force shrank. Yet there was no turning back. Once in retreat, they would be set upon by the unseen enemy and annihilated. The only direction they could follow was forward, toward Isker, the Khan's capital.

At last, in sight of the tent city, they rested for several days to gather strength. Then came the attack. It had to be victory at the first impact, or else the little band would be smothered by overwhelming numbers. Horses thundered forward; the glint of sabers reflected the rays of the sun as they approached the town, over which towered the silk and gold pavilion of the Khan.

They reined in the horses in utter astonishment. Eerie silence surrounded them. The city was deserted, except for women, children and old men. Following ancient Tatar tradition, the main force had withdrawn rather than face a determined enemy in open battle. Without losing a single warrior, Yermak planted his black standard in front of the Khan's pavilion. The Cossacks and Stroganov's men gave themselves over to days of looting and frolicking. Sibir was theirs.

A wagon train carrying pelts, gold and jewels was dispatched westward. Koltzo, now back in his chief's good graces, headed the escort. They brought the news of victory to the Stroganovs. Amidst the general rejoicing, Olga put on the necklace of rare jade which the hetman had sent her.

Koltzo continued his journey, and after several arduous weeks he arrived in Moscow. Upon hearing the message, the Czar took off his ermine cloak and draped it over the shoulders of the Cossack lieutenant. Nobody had received such an honor since a runner had brought him word of his first son's birth. No mention was made that technically the recipient, as well as his commander, were still outlaws with a price on their heads. All this was now forgotten. Yermak was assured of the Czar's gratitude, and the Stroganovs, Russia's foremost merchant princes, received even more generous privileges than they had possessed before.

In recent years, Moscow had had little cause for jubilation. News from the outside had more often than not been depressing. Now the city gave itself to days of unrestrained celebration. Church bells rang, men embraced and kissed in the streets and hymns of thanks rose to the heavens. In the year 1580 the word went from mouth to mouth: "God has bestowed a new Czardom on Russia."

Yermak himself did not return. A stupendous victory had been won, but it had to be consolidated. Winter was coming, and the victors were isolated in the unprotected city of Iskir, plagued by dwindling supplies and by marauding Tatar bands.

Ivan gave orders to a boyar general to lead a force of regulars to Yermak's assistance. A swift rider went ahead with the Czar's message of high praise and with a special royal gift, a set of armor made of finely wrought brass and gold emblazoned with the black double-headed eagle. The royal present arrived in good time, and Yermak immediately put on the costly breastplate. But the auxiliary force blundered along in confusion, not used to the fast riding pace and quick-acting tactics of the Cossacks. When they finally arrived in Iskir, they found the city still in Russian hands, but deep in mourning.

In the exuberance of victory, and pressed for food and winter clothing, Yermak had lost his sense of caution. After receiving reports that a large merchant caravan was approaching, he led a small contingent of his brothers to capture it. The report turned out to be a ruse. There was no caravan. Instead, the war party ran into a well-laid Tatar ambush. The Cossacks found themselves pinned down between the enemy and a wide river, on which their boats were riding tied to stout tree trunks.

The attack came in the middle of the night. The Cossacks

scampered to the safety of their boats. But Yermak, weighted down by the heavy armor, the Czar's gift, stumbled into the ice-cold water and drowned. The double-headed eagle killed the Cossack hero as the shaman had prophesied. When Olga learned the news, she mounted her horse and leaped from a cliff into the foaming Chusavaya River.

Yermak lived on in legends told from one end of the empire to the other. Even the Tatar enemies, who had long believed him to be charmed with eternal life, now honored him in their songs. He became their folk hero just as much as that of the Russians.

Ivan the Terrible had dreamed of carrying the double-eagle to the shores of the Baltic Sea and deep into the western lands. His dream ended in frustration, though it was never to be forgotten in later decades. But, almost by accident, he gained a new empire in the east. Through the foresight of the Stroganovs and the daring of Yermak and his Cossacks, the banner of Russia was planted in Siberia. The first foothold on Asian soil had been gained.

In succeeding years, even the Siberian Tatars were forced to give up their marauding ways. Inspired by the tales of Yermak's exploits, new generations of Cossacks penetrated deeper into the Asian forest, pushing the frontier even farther eastward, and in their wake followed hardy pioneers to carve out new homes in the silent vastness. Local tribes of nomadic hunters and fishermen, such as the Kazaks and Yakuts, were vanquished and made to bow to the scepter of the Czar.

Within a span of eighty years, an expanding Russia had reached the Pacific Ocean. Moscow now ruled over a landmass larger than any country in the world. Siberia—remote, rough in climate but of immeasurable richness in natural resources—became the instrument by which the nation projected itself into the forefront of world powers.

In the waning days of his reign, Ivan had opened a door which led to greatness and might.

14
DEATH *of a* SINNER

The body is exhausted, the spirit is sick. The cords of my soul and of my body have been stretched too tight, and there is no physician who can heal me. I waited for one capable of suffering and mourning with me, but nobody came forward to console me. They all returned evil for good and responded to all my love with hatred.

These lines read as if written by a tottering old poverty-stricken wretch, waiting for his end in some lone and miserable hut, avoided like the plague by other human beings. Actually they appear in the will of Ivan IV, drawn up when he was fifty-one. He was then the absolute despot over areas of such vastness that nobody could draw their boundaries with certainty. At any rate, the land he ruled was at least twice the size of his father's realm, and more territories waited in the distance to fall under Rurik rule—soil abounding in grass and trees, mountains bulging with minerals, land that beckoned the hunter, the logger and the plowman.

Though Ivan's spacious empire was still basically landlocked, his emissaries dealt on equal footing with popes and emperors. He was called the dear brother of kings who, until recently, had not even recognized that Russia was a state worth bothering about. The Tatars, once God's scourge of the faithful, proclaimed the Czar as their overlord. Instead of arrows and fire-brands, they now sent wagons heaped with furs and jewels into the capital.

Yet the autocrat and anointed of God felt lonely and helpless. His heart cried out for friendship and love, but those precious prizes seemed forever to elude him. The people who worked and lived in close proximity aroused his distrust, and he had sent many of them to death and destruction. Yet he longed for com-panions in whose presence he could let down his guard and relax.

For days he isolated himself in his gloomy chambers, brooding and bewailing his lot. Then he appeared among his clerks and relatives, wandering through the cold halls, lashing out in anger at servants, falling on his knees and bruising his forehead on the stone floors before the innumerable icons which hung in the corners of every room. The melancholy shadows cast by smoky oil lamps on the austere likenesses of Christ and the saints re-flected the despair in his heart.

The sickness was in his spirit, not in his body. Despite all the excesses, the sexual debaucheries, the heavy drinking and the arduous travels and pilgrimages, no serious illness had befallen him since the one in his early manhood which had caused the first painful rift with his trusted advisers. Yet as the stooped figure, wrapped in loose robes, shuffled through the palace, he looked like a man twenty or more years older than he really was.

Ivan was now married for the seventh, or as some would have it, for the fifth time. Maria Nagaya had recently borne him a son who was crying lustily in his cradle. But the persons to whom he felt closer than to anybody else were Irina, the wife of his son Feodor, and her brother Boris Godunov. They were to him, he said, "like the two fingers of my hand." The descendant of a Tatar family, Boris was able and ambitious. To some degree he filled the place once occupied by Adashev and Sylvester.

Feodor, the son, had grown older, but not wiser, a victim of a genetic deficiency and medical ignorance. He was obese and slow, with a perpetual idiotic grin on his childish face. His own father said of him in disgust: "The only occupation he is good for is not being czar, but being a bell ringer." Indeed, the prince's life ambition was to ring the bells in a monastery.

That left, among the immediate family, Ivan Ivanovich, the heir to the throne. In height and stature he closely resembled his father, and the two shared many tastes and inclinations. Like the older Ivan, the Czarevich possessed broad interests and a keen intelligence. He read whatever books he could get in book-starved Moscow and was even dabbling in the art of writing himself. Off and on he worked on the biography of a saint, one of the innumerable holy figures revered by the Orthodox Church.

The two Ivans could often be seen together. The son sat at his father's side at councils of state and at receptions of foreign dignitaries. He accompanied him on his travels. Together they had observed the rape of Novgorod, and side by side they had watched from a platform on Red Square the torturing and the execution of those who had displeased the Czar. Everybody sensed that, on the day when the crown changed heads, there would be no change in the basic character of monarchic rule. Everything would continue as before. So it appeared on the eve of the most tragic catastrophe to befall the life of Ivan IV.

The cause was trivial, and the whole incident would have amounted to nothing had it not been for the Czar's terrible temper, which at times caused him to lose all the restraints which rational human beings commonly possess.

As so often, the main meal had lasted long into the afternoon hours. The whole company had risen from the royal table heavy with food and wine.

"Why was my son Ivan absent from dinner?" the father asked Boris Godunov, who was at his side. "He should have asked my permission. Come with me to his quarters."

Boris followed his sovereign with a worried mind. Clearly the Czar was in a bad mood, and this could mean all sorts of trouble.

They walked through long corridors to the other end of the palace, where the crown prince's suite of rooms was located. There they found the younger Ivan in the company of his wife, who was then pregnant.

The Czar looked at his daughter-in-law. Something in the young matron's apparel aroused his displeasure. The exact cause has never been established with certainty. Perhaps she had disposed of her girdle to be more comfortable in her delicate condition. Or she may not have worn the required number of petticoats. Those were serious transgressions against the code of modesty among noble ladies. The Czar, who was known inside and outside Russia for his wanton adventures, could be very prudish concerning women who belonged to his household.

"Shame on you. Is this the way for a royal princess to dress?" he shouted. His tongue was heavy from the many cups of wine he had consumed during the long meal. "You look like a common woman of the street, not like a member of the Rurik family."

The princess burst into tears and ran to her husband, seeking his protection. The sight of the sobbing woman clinging to his son infuriated the older Ivan even further. "What kind of woman have you found here to bear a future czar?" he screamed. "Chase that wench into the street, where she belongs."

All his life the crown prince had played the part of the obedient son. Even now he wanted to avoid direct conflict, but he felt that he could not abandon his wife to such senseless fury. "Leave her alone, Father," he said quietly. Only the bulging veins on his forehead betrayed the emotion which coursed through his mind. "Just remember some of the women you have associated with in the past."

This apparently was the wrong thing to say to the half-drunk emperor. The father's voice shrieked in hot anger. The son, gradually losing his own temper, shouted back. It was the first quarrel between the two, and it became more heated and more vituperative with every fresh answer. Passion replaced reason until the son forgot all prudence. "What a good fighter you are against helpless women," he blurted out. "Why didn't you show such courage when you were fighting the Poles?"

The words stung the father where it hurt most. He knew, as did everybody, that his personal courage against outside enemies had never been exemplary, to say the least. The story of his struggle with Poland was one of frustration and humiliation, and he had not ceased to smart under this military failure.

"Why, you insolent misbegotten whelp," the Czar burst out hoarsely. Losing control over himself completely, he raised his dreaded staff with the heavy metal knob. He swung with all his might. Young Ivan sank to the floor bleeding profusely. A deep gash had opened on his forehead. Again and again the staff descended on the stricken man. The crazed father's roar of wounded pride could be heard through the palace. Boris Godunov stepped between the two, but all he could do was ward off one blow with his own body. He too sank to the floor bleeding. In a fit of madness, Ivan lashed out again, and this time he hit the son's temple so hard that the bones were heard to crack.

Only when the Czarevich sprawled on the blood-soaked floor unconscious did the father come to his senses. The staff dropped from his hand. He collapsed over the prostrate body screaming: "Oh God, what have I done? I have killed my child."

He shouted for doctors, for bandages, for priests. Courtiers and servants who had heard the screams came running. They stood aghast before the spectacle of sudden stark tragedy. There was no doubt in anyone's mind that the Czarevich was dying, murdered by his own father.

For four days his life flickered on, though he never regained consciousness. Then it was over. As the Czar had lost all self-control in anger, so he now knew no restraint in his remorse. He held the lifeless body in his arms. "Don't leave me," he wailed. "Forgive me. I cannot forgive myself."

Day and night he crouched by the open coffin until monks

came to carry it away to the Cathedral of the Archangel Michael. As the body was lowered into the vault, the father threw himself on it. His cries of despair could be heard far beyond the walls of the sanctuary.

Ivan never recovered. He was like a broken pillar, like a tree felled by lightning. No food touched his lips for days. Raving and babbling unintelligible sounds, he wandered through the halls. When he encountered a member of his court, he lashed out at him with his cursed staff, but a moment later he would fling himself at the feet of the attacked to beg his forgiveness. Those who had once feared him now pitied the pathetic figure ravaged by guilt and self-torture.

The playwright Alexei Tolstoy has the penitent Ivan cry out in anguish:

> I allowed the devil to rule my deathless soul.
> I am no Czar, rather a wolf, a cur.
> I have loved tortures and torments. I slew
> My son, a crime greater than the guilt
> Of Cain himself. I am in mind and soul
> A man of sin. My heart's iniquities
> Cannot be numbered by man's feeble powers.

No excess of self-torture could bring the dead back to life, but the wounds which were not fatal could heal with time. Humbly Ivan made his way to the chamber where Boris Godunov lay on his sickbed. He begged the wounded man's forgiveness and ordered that everything possible be done to make him comfortable. The injury turned out to be less dangerous than it appeared at first, and Boris made a complete recovery.

The whole country was stunned by the tragedy. Russians everywhere took it as a major national calamity, akin to a plague or an enemy invasion. But there was hardly any condemnation of the one who had perpetrated the deed. It was God's arm that had struck down the heir to the throne; the father was merely His instrument. They shared the Czar's sorrow and wept with him over his loss.

It was more than a personal loss. Ivan's whole life had been spent overcoming the fragmentation of Russia which the princes and boyars desired. He had come closer than any predecessor to building up a strong, centralized monarchy. The vision of a great, unified nation was approaching reality, and the son was to carry on, to assure continuity. Now the whole edifice of the aging Czar's hopes and aspirations was collapsing around him.

With a stroke of his gilded cudgel Ivan had virtually wiped out the Rurik dynasty. Feodor, the second son, now twenty-one years old, was not fit to be czar. The only other legitimate son was the baby Dmitri, and even his legitimacy was in question, since the father's later marriages did not conform to the church code.

The plan of succession was as dead as the successor himself. A substitute plan, however poor, had to be devised. Ivan drew up a new will naming Feodor the next Czar, but stipulating that Boris Godunov would be his chief adviser. The mentally defective son would rule in name and his capable brother-in-law in reality.

In his final days, Ivan, the butcher of Novgorod and scourge of the boyar class, became almost gentle. The wolf sounded more like a lamb. There were no more executions. Blood ceased to flow, and the gallows on Red Square stood unused. Ivan's final will contains this advice to his successor:

Rule with love, avoid war against Christian nations. Give thought to the relief of your people so they will not suffer burdensome taxes or the hardships they had to endure under my reign. Honor my memory by freeing the prisoners of war from their bonds.

Once so full of zest and vitality, Ivan the Terrible had lost the will to live. Again and again he spoke of retiring to a monastery to spend his remaining days in exercises of penitence. Only occasionally did the old drive break through the pall of despair. Then he busied himself feverishly with the details of the Polish armistice, the activities of the British traders and the consolidation of the Siberian conquests.

Inexorably, the strength of a life squandered in excesses and in self-destruction was ebbing away. In the winter of 1584, a dreadful illness befell the Czar. His weakened body gave out an unbearable stench. Not even the English physician in whom he had so much trust knew of a diagnosis, much less a cure.

When science conceded defeat, the call went out for supernatural help. In all the monasteries, from the southern steppes to the shores of the White Sea, prayers were offered for the stricken sovereign. The common folk crowded into the churches and lighted countless little candles.

Miracle-working icons were carried into the sickroom by monks, who took turns chanting in behalf of the Czar's soul. With them came magicians from near and far. They called for the unicorn's horn and for dragon's milk, and they drew circles on a flat table into which live spiders were released. When the creatures died quickly, the wise men shook their heads in dismay. It was a bad omen.

In the middle of the night, a servant shouted: "A comet is in the sky. God have mercy on us all." With groans of pain the patient rose and dragged himself to the head of the red staircase over which he had so often descended to banquets and formal audiences. Clutching the marble banister with bony fingers, he looked out at the dark sky. There it was over the bell tower, a reddish star with a long, glimmering tail. "It is announcing my death," moaned the sick man, collapsing at the landing. Hurriedly the servants carried him back to his bed.

The soothsayers bent over their sticks and bones. They shook and rattled them and then let them drop on the floor. For a long time they studied the figures the objects had formed in falling. Then the oldest among them proclaimed, "Death will come on the eighteenth of March."

It did not take a prophet's foresight to know that the end was near. The dying man was clinging to the last shred of life. His old meanness broke through once more as he threatened the soothsayers. "If I am still alive after that day, you will all die."

The high church and court dignitaries who filled the room tried hard not to notice the putrid smell. In a voice which was barely audible, Ivan called for his personal treasure. Chests of teakwood were hurriedly carried up from the underground vaults and emptied beside the dying man. The trembling fingers sifted through the mounds of pearls and rubies, golden bracelets and diamond-studded pins. In a gesture of futility he pushed the now useless trinkets away and called for his chessboard.

He had always excelled in this, the Russian national game. His superior reasoning power made him a formidable opponent, even when fearful subordinates did not take the precaution of letting the chief win. With a wave of the hand he challenged Boris Godunov to oppose him in the game. The thirty-two chessmen, carved from ivory and inlaid with diamonds, were set up on the black and white squares. The game began. But as soon as Ivan touched the king to move him from his original place, he sank back on the cushion. The ivory king clattered to the floor. The game was over.

In his last delirious moments, Ivan called to the son whom he had killed. He seemed to see him by his side, and he talked to him in endearing terms until his lips ceased to move. It was the evening of March 18, 1584.

Hurriedly the Metropolitan, Dionysius, stepped to the bedside and performed the ceremony which the living Ivan had so often desired, but never strongly enough to go through with. A monk's black habit was draped over the lifeless figure, and a circular space, a tonsure, was cut into the gray hair on the dead Czar's head. The cleric chanted the formula of monastic consecration. In death, Ivan the Terrible, Czar of all Russia, Prince of Moscow, Tver, Novgorod, Kazan, Astrakhan and Sibir, became Jonah, a simple monk of the Holy Orthodox Church, owning nothing but the black cassock on his stiffening body.

15

TIME *of* TROUBLE

"*Gospodi pomilui*—Lord, have mercy on us," chanted the monks as they bore the body of Ivan Vasilevich to its resting place. Though the remains were clad in the habit of a simple monk, the funeral was held with the grandeur due the autocratic monarch of a mighty empire. Behind the coffin strode the heir apparent, Feodor, a foolish grin on his face, leaning heavily on the arm of Boris Godunov, whose regal bearing was noticed with glances of admiration by the crowd which filled the square.

The riderless horse of the late Czar was led by his personal groom. Slowly the princes and boyars, the serving gentry, the Englishmen of the Russia Company and the leaders of the merchants' and craftsmen's guilds marched along.

"*Gospodi pomilui*," murmured Prince Boris Godunov, and he remembered the day when the younger Ivan lay dying in his father's arms. The Czar's spirit had been filled not only with the deepest remorse, but with visions of doom for himself, his immortal soul and the whole nation. "All is lost," the anguished man had cried out. "All I have built is destroyed. Nothing is left."

Boris' mind was burdened with forebodings of doom, and as he looked around at the masses of mourners he felt that they too shared his feeling of impending tragedy. Their sorrow was deep and sincere. They mourned for the man Ivan, the bearer of Monomach's crown, but they also remembered the bloody comet which had streaked across the pale skies of Moscow so shortly before his death. It was a warning of evil days to come.

The premonitions were to prove correct. Only a few years after Russia's first Czar had been entombed beside his father and his slain son, the most tragic period in the history of the nation opened. It nearly brought about the complete collapse of the structure which Ivan IV and before him his ancestors had so assiduously built. Very aptly, historians have named this period the Time of Trouble.

Severe trouble, however, did not set in immediately at the death of Ivan the Terrible. For a while, the machinery of state kept on turning fairly smoothly. Feodor Ivanovich had inherited none of his father's qualities except a childlike piety. He spent most of his time visiting monasteries, where he was allowed to ring the bells to his heart's content. As for matters of government, neither did they interest him nor could his defective mind understand them.

He was perfectly satisfied to leave those matters to his brother-in-law, Boris Godunov, who turned out to be a skillful diplomat and an able administrator. By and large, Boris followed the course charted by Ivan IV but without the excesses and the outbursts of destructive temper which had blemished Ivan's record. While the peasantry and the middle class were relieved, there was dismay among the princes and boyars. They had hoped that with the death of their archenemy, the good old days would immediately return, the days when they lorded it over their lands, unrestricted by royal power. But for the time being, Boris was firmly in the saddle, and so they bided their time. Soon it came.

Czar Feodor died in 1598. Hardly anybody was greatly surprised by his comparatively early demise. Those who knew him personally were aware of his weak constitution. His skin had a sallow, unhealthy look. His body was encased in layers of fat, with muscles so puny that he walked with difficulty. He had certainly not been an asset to his exalted position, yet as long as he lived, he had performed one useful service: his signature of approval had given Boris Godunov's work the stamp of legality. While the edicts issued forth from the Kremlin in the name of the duly anointed Czar, nobody dared raise his voice in objection. Now the situation was changed.

Perhaps Boris could have arranged a similar relationship with Dmitri, the son of Ivan's seventh wife and the last male descendant of the Rurik line, but Dmitri was dead, or so it had been announced in 1591. The widowed mother had taken the infant with her to Uglich, a remote provincial town, and nobody had ever seen him alive again.

When persons with claims to a throne die of unexplained causes, talk of poison begins to circulate quickly. First there were only whispers, but after Feodor's death, the boyars spread the word gleefully until it was told and retold from the Gulf of Finland to Siberia that Boris Godunov had been the one to dispatch little Dmitri to his eternal repose.

The story did not make much sense, since Boris would have been better off as regent under a child czar, but this did not prevent his enemies from trying to destroy his reputation.

When the rumors swelled to a shrill chorus, Boris hastily convened the *Zemski Sobor*. This assembly of notables had not met for decades. Using all the pressure which he as the de facto ruler could bring to bear, he managed to silence the opposition. The majority of the assembly acclaimed him the next Czar. Now he could enjoy all the honors and wear all the paraphernalia of an office which had already for all practical purposes been his for some time.

But the years of inner peace were over. The high aristocracy saw no more reason for restraint. Boris was denounced as a usurper, an unworthy upstart of Tatar origin. Despite all his unquestioned ability, he could not claim the aura of holiness, of divine ordination, which had surrounded the house of Rurik. The long-frustrated nobility grasped at the chance to throw off the yoke which Ivan the Terrible had laid on them.

Civil war rent the empire asunder, and as always when internal trouble weakens a nation, outsiders found excuses to profit from its difficulties. The Poles renewed their old enmity, assisted by dissident Cossack bands in quest of easy booty. Tatar chiefs in the south and in the east became restless once more, encouraged by the Sultan of Turkey, who bade them make as much mischief as they could.

Trying desperately to fight the enemies at the borders and the adversaries inside his realm at the same time, Czar Boris ruined his health. He died in 1605.

What followed were years of total anarchy. The armies which roamed the country resembled hordes of brigands more than regular fighting forces. A number of boyar factions, with their armed retainers, attacked and ambushed each other. Nobles with well-known names switched sides so frequently in the confused struggle that they were mockingly called "birds of passage." Mobs raged through the merchant quarters of Moscow, looting and burning at will. The misery of the common man was compounded by several years of poor harvests, which brought widespread famine in their wake.

Even though the bodies of the Ruriks were now entombed in the Cathedral of the Archangel Michael, their ghosts were not allowed to rest. Persistent stories went around towns and villages that Dmitri, the youngest son of Ivan IV, was not dead at all. At the supposed burial of the Czarevich the body of another child had been substituted. Twice within short intervals, false Dmitris appeared in the country, adventurous impostors in each case, and both times they attracted large followings and were boosted by outside enemies. They marched against Moscow to claim the crown of Monomach and were only beaten back after heavy and costly fighting.

Not until 1613 was it possible to convene another *Zemski Sobor* for the purpose of ending the chaos. By that time, everybody agreed that, to save the nation, orderly government had to be reinstated. As on previous occasions, the nobility and the clergy were predominant in this august assembly, but it also contained a sprinkling of the more prosperous merchants—and, as a momentous innovation, some representatives of the peasantry had been admitted.

The debate over the choice of a suitable ruler was long and bitter. Many names were proposed, only to be rejected by one or another faction. Any strong or popular personality was out as far as the boyars were concerned. A czar who was a nonentity, who would leave them to their own devices, was the only kind that would suit them. But even they were reluctant to nominate anybody who had no ties whatsoever with the former ruling house. The search was on for a man who could claim such ties and at the same time remain rather inconspicuous. Representatives of the lower classes especially felt very strongly that some sort of continuity should be preserved. God's blessing, it was felt, would be with a person related, in some fashion, with the exalted Rurik house.

After a long search a candidate was finally located who pleased nearly everybody. Michael Romanov was practically unknown anywhere, except within a small circle of friends. He had never shown any ambition to wield power, but he possessed an all-important qualification: as a nephew of the late Anastasia, Ivan's first wife, he was related to the Czar, though not very closely.

And so the Romanov dynasty entered history. Order was eventually restored, and the Romanovs ruled in the splendor which Ivan Grozni had craved so ardently throughout his reign. Strong, undiluted absolutism was their system. All Russians, noble and lowborn, had to bow to their will, and this included the clergy of the Holy Orthodox Church, married parish priests as well as the celibate monks who were the only ones eligible to rise to the rank of bishop or even higher. The church crowned the Romanov czars in majestic rites, but once the crown sat securely on the ruler's brow, bishops, archbishops and metropolitans submitted to his dictates. When rebellion finally arose against the czarist regime, the rebels also turned on the Orthodox clergy, which stood accused of helping tyranny maintain itself in power rather than ministering to the poor and to the suppressed.

In the days of Ivan the Terrible, the highest Russian churchman bore the title of metropolitan. But in the year 1589, this title was replaced by the even more exalted one of patriarch. Heretofore the Metropolitans of Moscow had honored the Patriarch of Constantinople as their spiritual superior; now the Patriarch of Moscow was his equal in rank, and in actual importance he surpassed him by far. Constantinople had become a largely Muslim city and the capital of a Muslim empire. Its patriarch presided only over a small minority of the population in his own country; but the Patriarch of Moscow was now the leading ecclesiastic in a rapidly expanding empire in which Eastern Orthodoxy was not only the religion of the majority, but also the privileged state religion. In a very real sense the sprawling settlement on the banks of the Moskva River had become the Third Rome.

Blessed and aided by the church, presenting themselves to the people as God's representatives, the Romanov czars continued what Ivan had begun. He had set out for goals still beyond his strength, but his successors reached them. Gradually the eastern boundaries were pushed to the inhospitable shores of the Pacific, to the gates of China and into the same endless steppes which once were the home grounds of the feared Turkish and Mongolian conquerors. Across the Bering Strait Russian explorers made their way to the American continent, and in their wake came hardy Russian fur traders.

The "window to the Baltic," which had remained barred to Ivan the Terrible, was eventually wrenched wide open by Peter the Great (1682–1725). This remarkable disciple of the Rurik czar also shared Ivan's admiration of Western cultural and technical achievements. His new capital, St. Petersburg near the Baltic, was proudly proclaimed by its residents to be the Venice or the Paris of the north, both for its architectural decor and for its refined intellectual life.

The Ottoman Turk, once dreaded in orient and occident, had become the "sick man of Europe." The sultanate was a helpless decaying corpse from which greedy neighbors were tearing pieces of flesh, and thereby getting in each other's way. Russia received the major spoils in this gruesome contest.

Fleets flying the double-eagle began to venture from Russian ports on the Baltic and on the Black Sea into the open ocean. Poland and Lithuania, which Ivan had coveted in vain, ceased to exist as independent powers.

Authoritarian rule was the lot of the Russian people in the days of the first czar; it continued in the age of the Romanovs, and it is still firmly entrenched under the sign of the hammer and sickle. Ivan the Terrible was the model of the supreme autocrat for the Romanovs and later for such Soviet leaders as Joseph Stalin. Ivan's *oprichniki* remind us of their counterparts in the various secret police organizations which were maintained by the Romanovs and, after 1917, by the Bolshevik regime.

If there is such a thing as the spirit of Russia, Ivan the Terrible represented it at its best and at its worst. His mind possessed some of the brilliance found in so many scholars and diplomats of his nation. In the works of the famous writers in nineteenth-century Russia, we can detect something akin to his brooding melancholy, which is perhaps induced by the long harsh winters and the immense spaces of the endless plains. His painful mysticism, his continuous self-searching and self-reproach is echoed in the great books of Leo Tolstoi, Feodor Dostoevski and others.

Because so much of Ivan's personality was typically Russian, the common people could identify with him, and he retained their sympathy despite all his transgressions. Reinhold Heider-stain, a German who served in Ivan's army, observed:

Those who study the history of his reign should be surprised that in spite of his cruelty, the people should love him so strongly with a love that other sovereigns can acquire only by indulgence and kindness, and that their extraordinary devotion to their sovereign could last so long.

For the Russian people, Ivan was the hero of Kazan, the conqueror of Siberia, the prince who had led them toward greatness. For the poor he was the scourge of their cruel landlords, and for everybody he was the right arm of the Lord Himself.

Strolling singers and balladeers embellished his deeds until he became a legend, likened to Alexander and Caesar, whose descendant he claimed to be. The legend persisted until 1917, when the Bolshevik revolution consigned him, together with all other czars, to oblivion. But in later decades he was pardoned and rehabilitated. Now Russian children learn in school about Ivan Grozni, the defender of the poor, and in a Russian-made motion picture of giant proportions he was featured as the great national superhero, with hardly a blemish attached to his character.

Ivan IV was a person of rare gifts and of a rare sensitivity, but the odds were heavily stacked against him from early childhood. Frustration was his constant companion; it had to be, since his vision of power was not upheld by reality. He was a man constantly pursued and constantly pursuing, a reformer whose reforms were premature in his particular setting, a tragic figure, tragic in his own lifetime and afterward, because biographers and chroniclers have not been kind to him.

Very few original documents concerning his life and work have been preserved, and so historical research must depend on circumstantial evidence and intelligent guesswork. Official records and most of what Ivan wrote down himself have perished in the frequent Moscow fires. What remains as historical source material are the denunciations of his personal enemies, such as Kurbsky, which must be taken with several grains of salt. Nobody seriously thinks that, even had all the records been salvaged, he would appear as an innocent angel. But we can reasonably assume that, in his violence and lack of human compassion, he was no worse than many other high-born contemporaries in a most violent period of man's history. But the others escaped the damning epithet "The Terrible," which he bears to this day.

THE LAST GRAND PRINCES OF MOSCOW

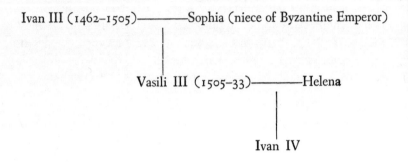

Ivan III (1462–1505)————Sophia (niece of Byzantine Emperor)

Vasili III (1505–33)————Helena

Ivan IV

THE FIRST CZARS OF RUSSIA

Ivan the Terrible (1533–84)————Anastasia

Feodor I (1584–98)

Boris Godunov (1598–1605)

Time of Trouble (1605–13)

Michael Romanov (1613–45)

CHRONOLOGICAL TABLE

(Events outside the Russian area appear in italics)

907–1169	Principality of Kiev
1242–1462	Mongol invasions; Golden Horde
1440	*Gutenberg invents printing press*
1453	*Ottoman Turks conquer Constantinople*
1462–1505	Ivan III, Grand Prince of Moscow
1480	Ivan III refuses tribute to Golden Horde
1492	*Columbus discovers America*
1505–33	Vasili III, Grand Prince of Moscow
1517	*Luther's 95 Theses*
1530	Ivan the Terrible born
1533	Ivan becomes Grand Prince of Moscow
1538	Death of Queen Mother Helena
1547	Ivan crowned Czar of Russia; marries Anastasia Zakharin-Romanov
1552	Conquest of Kazan
1553	Ivan's illness
	Death of Czarevich Dmitri
	British open White Sea trade route
1554	Czarevich Ivan born
1557	Astrakhan conquered
	Livonian war begins
1558	*Elizabeth becomes Queen of England*
1560	Death of Anastasia
1564	*Galileo and Shakespeare born*
	Founding of Oprichnina
	Kurbsky deserts
1568	Land grant to Stroganov family
1570	Punishment of Novgorod
1571	Crimean Tatars burn Moscow
1574–86	*Stephen Batory, King of Poland*
1575–77	"Czar" Simeon
1580	Pope Gregory XIII sends legate to mediate between Russia and Poland; Cossack leader Yermak captures capital of Sibir
1581	Serfdom fully established; Ivan's seventh wife gives birth to Prince Dmitri
1582	Ivan kills his oldest son; Armistice with Poland
1584	Death of Ivan the Terrible
1584–98	Czar Feodor; regency of Boris Godunov
1588	*British sea victory over Spanish Armada*
1589	First Patriarch of Moscow
1598–1605	Czar Boris Godunov
1605–13	"Time of Trouble"
1613	Michael Romanov becomes Czar

185

SUGGESTED FURTHER READINGS

Baker, George. *The Deadly Parallel: Stalin and Ivan the Terrible.* New York: Random House, 1950.

Clarkson, Jesse D. *A History of Russia, 2nd ed.* New York: Random House, 1969.

Dmytryshyn, Basil, ed. *Medieval Russia: A Sourcebook.* New York: Holt, Rinehart & Winston, 1967.

Eckhardt, Hans von. *Ivan the Terrible.* New York: A. A. Knopf, 1949.

Fennell, J. L. I., tr. and ed. *The Correspondence between Prince A. M. Kurbsky and Czar Ivan IV of Russia.* Cambridge, England: Cambridge University Press, 1955.

Fennell, J. L. I., ed. *Prince A. M. Kurbsky's History of Ivan IV.* Cambridge, England: Cambridge University Press, 1965.

Florinsky, Michael T., ed. *Encyclopedia of Russia and the Soviet Union.* New York: McGraw-Hill, 1961.

Graham, Stephen. *Ivan the Terrible.* New Haven, Conn.: Yale University Press, 1933.

Grey, Ian. *Ivan the Terrible.* Philadelphia: Lippincott, 1964.

Harcave, Sidney. *Russia: A History, 4th ed.* Philadelphia: Lippincott, 1959.

Koslow, Jules. *Ivan the Terrible.* New York: Hill & Wang, 1962.

Lamb, Harold. *The March of Muscovy.* Garden City, N.Y.: Doubleday, 1951.

Outline History of the U.S.S.R. Moscow: Foreign Language Publishing House, 1960.

Riha, Thomas, ed. *Readings in Russian Civilization.* Chicago: University of Chicago Press, 1964.

Spector, Ivar. *An Introduction to Russian History and Culture, 2nd ed.* Princeton, N.J.: Van Nostrand, 1954.

Tolstoi, A. K. *The Death of Ivan the Terrible* (drama). G. R. Noyes, ed., in *Masterpieces of the Russian Drama*, vol. 2. New York: Dover, 1933.

Von Staden, Heinrich. *The Land and Government of Muscovy: A Sixteenth Century Account.* Palo Alto, Calif.: Stanford University Press, 1967.

Waliszewski, K. *Ivan the Terrible.* Hamden, Conn.: Archon Books, 1966.

Whipper, R. *Ivan Grozni.* Moscow: Foreign Language Publishing House, 1947.

INDEX

ABOUT THE AUTHOR

Alfred Apsler was born in Vienna, Austria in 1907 and is now an American citizen. He began writing in his student years, and has been a contributor to newspapers and magazines in Europe and the United States and author of trade books and textbooks. Since 1943 he has taught in high schools and colleges in Oregon and Washington. At present he is professor of social science and history at Clark College in Vancouver, Washington, where he lives with his wife. He has two grown children.